DOGSTEPS
Illustrated gait at a glance

DOGSTEPS

Illustrated Gait at a Glance

by RACHEL PAGE ELLIOTT

*Illustrations by Eve Andrade
and the author*

Seventh Printing—1981
HOWELL BOOK HOUSE Inc.
230 Park Avenue
New York, N.Y. 10169

Copyright © 1973 by Howell Book House Inc.

Library of Congress Catalog Card No. 72-182242
ISBN 0-87605-519-6

No part of this book may be reproduced
without permission in writing from the publisher.

Printed in U.S.A.

*To my husband,
whose patience made it possible.*

Contents

Foreword   9

Author's Introduction   11

1. Common Terms and Comparative Skeletons   15
   Terms must be understood to be meaningful.

2. The Natural Gaits . . .   21
   Gait Patterns Defined

3. Good Performance Is the Test of Good Structure   33
   Why dogs need sound structure; how function can influence form.

4. Angulation and Balance—   43
   Foundation of Structure and Movement
   The importance of angulation; the value of balance; how angulation affects muscle structure; hints on determining shoulder layback.

5. Heads and Tails—and Other Views   61
   Semantics and optical illusion cause confusion in understanding dog gait; the normal stance; normal and faulty action; why dogs pace; detrimental effects of the tight lead; how do we look to others?

Conclusion   92

Bibliography   94

References   95

Foreword

THERE has long been need for understandable information on various points of great concern to dog breeders.

Too often, people supervise breeding of dogs without knowledge of what they are doing to the breed from an hereditary standpoint. Of the many faults that can be produced, probably the most obvious are those which contribute to lameness or poor gait.

Mrs. Elliott has recognized this need for education of dog breeders in the basics of sound gait and performance. Based upon her years of association with show and field trial dogs, study of reel after reel of movie film, and the application of her findings to her own dogs, she has prepared this fine book.

It is especially aimed for the layman, with clear simple wording and easy-to-understand drawings. Study of this material will aid all in recognizing what is good and what is faulty action, and the application of what is learned should produce rewarding results for the conscientious dog breeder.

I compliment Mrs. Elliott for her deep insight into problems, her tireless work, and her devotion to improvement of dog breeds by careful selection of parents. I hope this high quality book will be the first of a series clearly showing what can be achieved by proper breeding of dogs.

—E. W. TUCKER, D.V.M.

(Dr. Tucker is a past president of the American Veterinary Medical Association, and of the Massachusetts Veterinary Association.)

Acknowledgments

I SHOULD like to express appreciation to my good friends who have helped—directly or indirectly—in the compilation of this material, and whose interest and encouragement have contributed so much to bringing the book to completion.

Special thanks go to my son-in-law, Maris Platais, professional artist, for his wise counsel, and to Eve Andrade, whose pencil drawings of dogs at work have brought life to the text. I wish to especially thank my sister, Priscilla Rose, for valuable suggestions, and publisher Elsworth Howell for tactful and constructive guidance. Thanks are due, too, to Dr. Edgar Tucker of the Concord Animal Hospital, whose dedication to the need for education among the dog laity, in the interest of sounder dogs, has been a constant source of inspiration and challenge.

—RACHEL PAGE ELLIOTT

Author's Introduction

This book is a concise, illustrated introduction to the subject of gait, designed to make easier the recognition of normal and faulty ways in which the dog moves.

Gait tells much about a dog's structure that is not revealed when he is standing still, for it reflects his physical coordination, balance of body and soundness. The correlation between gait and structure is frequently misunderstood, and—in a time when growing interest in dogs as family pets tends to lessen awareness of the need for stamina and working ability—its significance is often overlooked.

Sound movement contributes to the health and normal lifespan of all dogs. It is as desirable a feature in the family pet as it is important to the usefulness of dogs bred for hunting, farm work, police duty or racing; and without it, show winners can never achieve true excellence. Also, sound dogs are happier dogs. This emphasis is not to detract from the value of type and temperament, which are necessary for the preservation of any breed, but rather to underline the truth of the old saying, "As a dog moves, so is he built."

All dogs do not gait alike. Differences in size and shape influence their way of going. The flashy step of a small terrier, for example, or the brisk trot of a Welsh Corgi, is not the same as the easy, loose stride of Bloodhounds or Newfoundlands. And the spirited drive of proud-headed Setters lends contrast to the patient scent-trailing action of Basset Hounds. Through the centuries, man has developed various kinds of dogs to meet his needs and his fancies, and their individuality today is the result of long years of selective breeding.

Varied as dogs are, however, the principle by which they cover the ground is the same for all and is dictated by nature. This is the law of balance and gravity, which is constantly directed toward efficient forward motion with a minimum waste of effort—the key to good movement. When man upsets this law through inattention to sound structure, nature has to compensate for his mistakes with counter-balances which show up in faulty gaiting patterns.

Incorrect movement, either temporary or permanent, can also occur as a result of lameness due to sprains, breaks, cuts, bruises or other reasons, but these should be recognized for what they are and not confused with inherited defects. Faults vary in severity and frequency from dog to dog, and from breed to breed, but they are universal to the canine world—constantly challenging our search for perfection.

While one does not have to be a student of anatomy to appreciate dogs, the ability to recognize good and poor movement is basic for a working knowledge. To be sure, movement is quicker than the eye, but the educated eye knows better what to look for, and the eye that understands is not easily deceived. In the course of my study on this subject, I have taken slow-motion movies, from which I have drawn animated sequences showing various phases of leg action at different angles to the viewer. Included, also, are a few skeletal suggestions to help the reader visualize bone and joint movement beneath coat and muscles. Some of the illustrations may appear to be exaggerated—actually, they are not.

The models for discussion were selected at random solely for analysis and study, and there is no intention to associate any of the technical sketches with a particular breed—for all are vulnerable. Except for some of the pencil drawings showing dogs at work, most of the studies portray dogs moving at the trot, as this gait is generally considered best for evaluating movement as it relates to build. However, some examples of other gaits have also been included for identification and comparison.

For newcomers, interest in DOGSTEPS may be simply in owning a good dog. Nevertheless, we hope there is something of value here for *all* dog fanciers, and particularly the many breeders who are striving to raise better puppies.

Code to the gait diagrams in this book:

Front paw —

Rear paw —

Paws connected with dotted lines move as a pair.

Sample:

The Pace

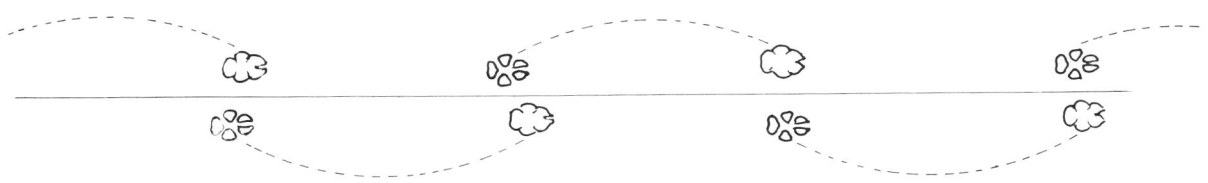

1.

Common Terms and Comparative Skeletons

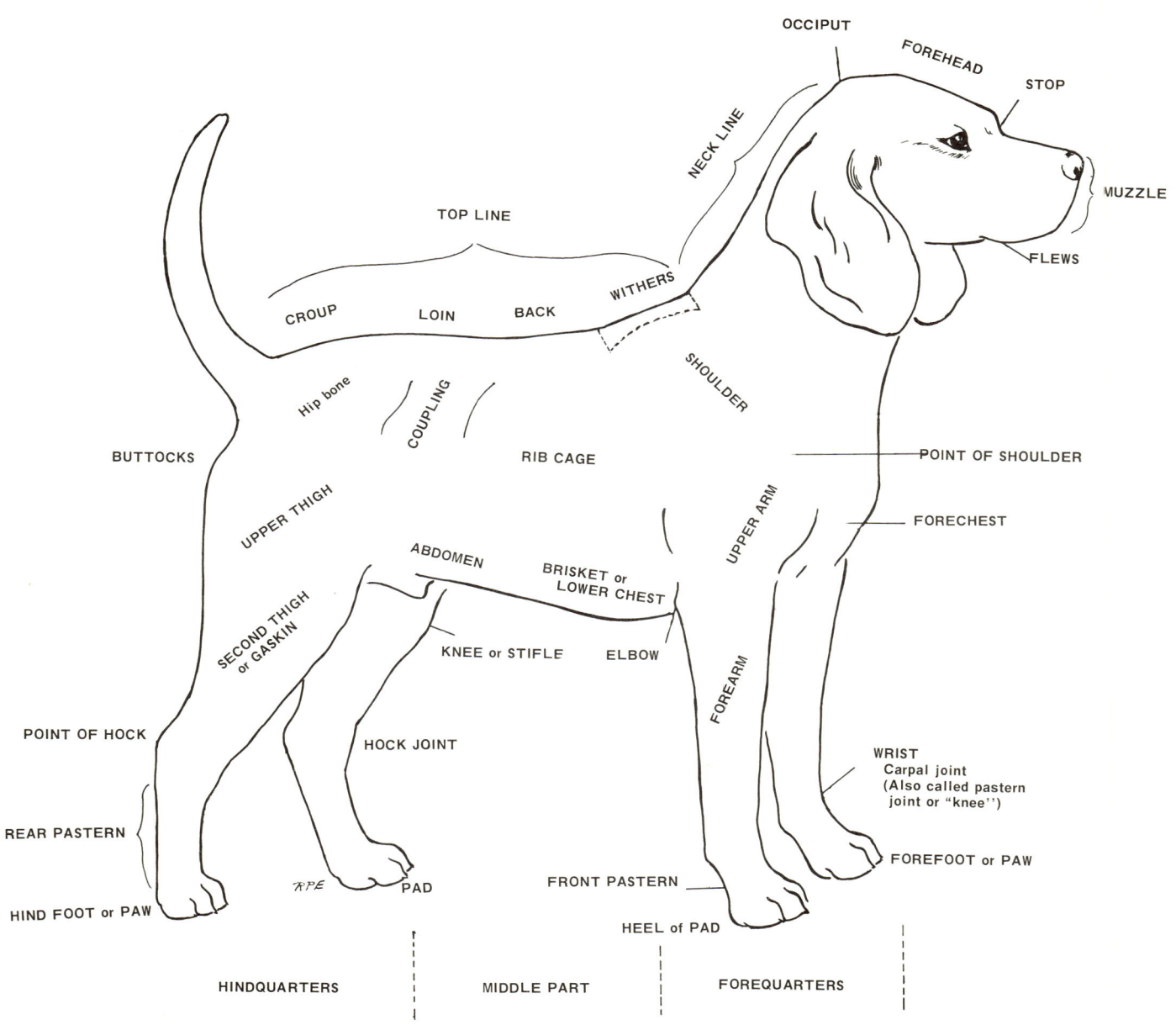

Terms Must Be Understood to Be Meaningful

To MAKE certain that we are all speaking the same language in the pages that follow, skeletal diagrams of the dog, the horse, and man are included here. Basically, the nomenclature pertaining to dogs comes from the paddock, and though some of the terms have become misconstrued and ambiguous due to the widening gap between horse and dog followers, most of the parlance common to both interests remains intact. Structurally, horses and dogs share much in common, and the principles that apply to gait and to sound conformation are practically the same for both.

Personal experience and meaningful associations often influence terminology. Thus, some anatomists prefer to relate parts of the dog with comparable parts of man, rather than with the horse—no doubt because they have lacked the opportunity for first-hand acquaintance with horses. As examples, they term the carpal joint the wrist (instead of "knee" or pastern), identify the hock as heel, and—because the dog is actually a toe-walker—insist on use of the term "paw" rather than "foot". In their terminology, foot is label for the rear leg from hock to toes. This is not to say who is right or who is wrong, but I think it easier to avoid misunderstandings about the lower extremities if we accept the definition from Webster's dictionary which describes the foot as "that part of an animal upon which it rests when standing, or upon which it moves."

Newcomers to the dog game may be perplexed by the double meanings and interchange of terms which are heard from time to time, but fortunately the confusion is something we can get accustomed to as we gain understanding of what is meant. Matters of more serious concern, however, are the misleading and conflicting references which relate to the way dogs should or should not move. Mindful of the foregoing comments, readers are urged to look into the works on anatomy and animal locomotion listed on page 95, any one of which would be an interesting addition to a dog owner's library.

Comparative Skeletal Diagrams—

Showing commonly-used canine terms that derive from both horse and man, including a few scientific references:

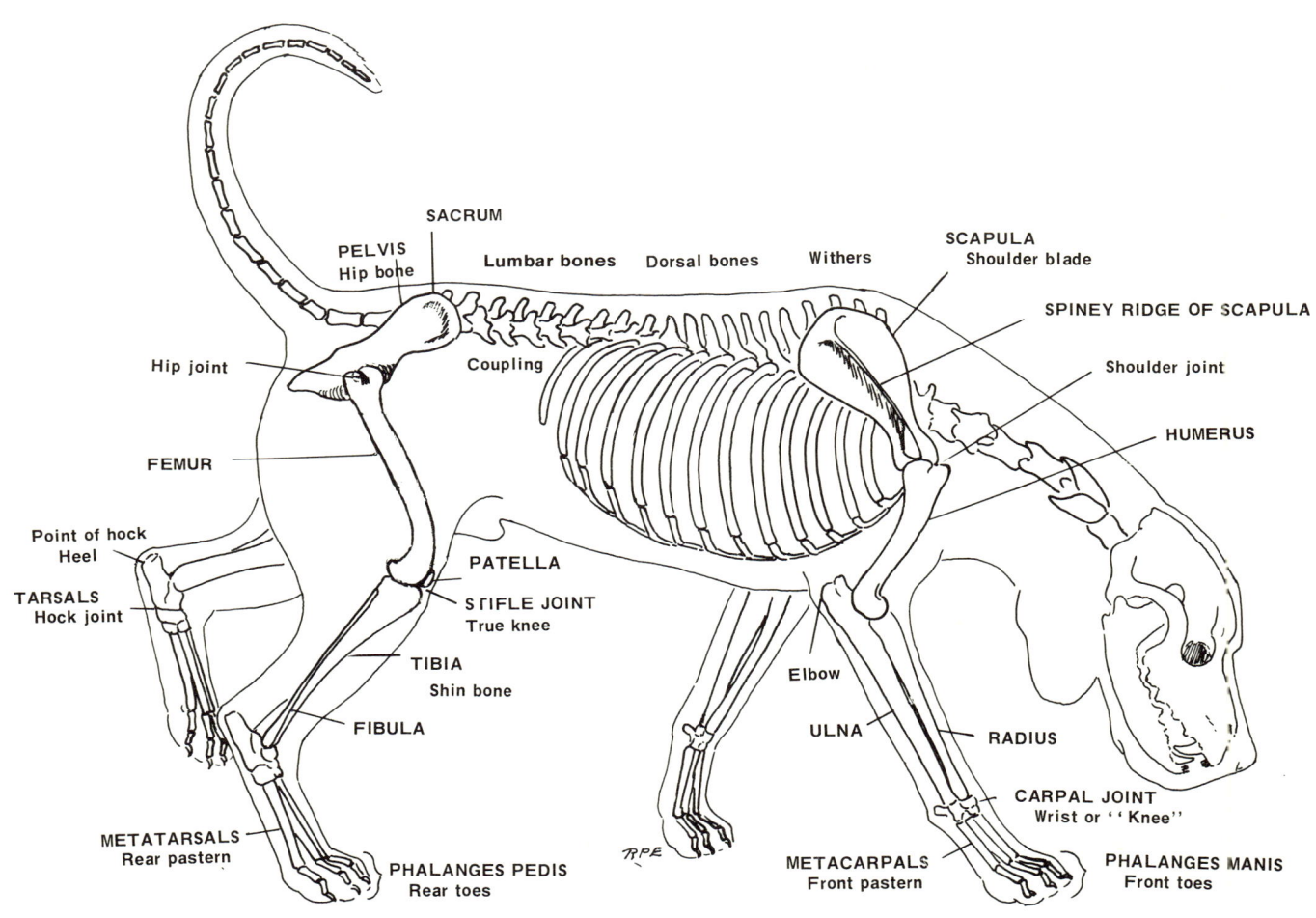

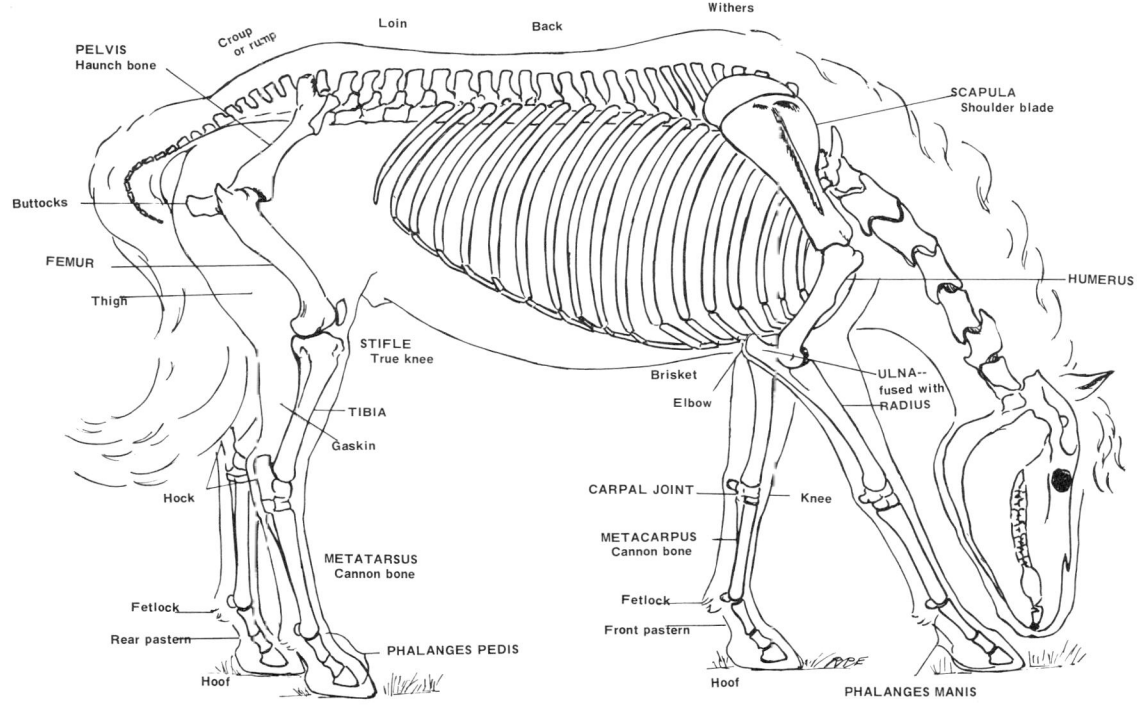

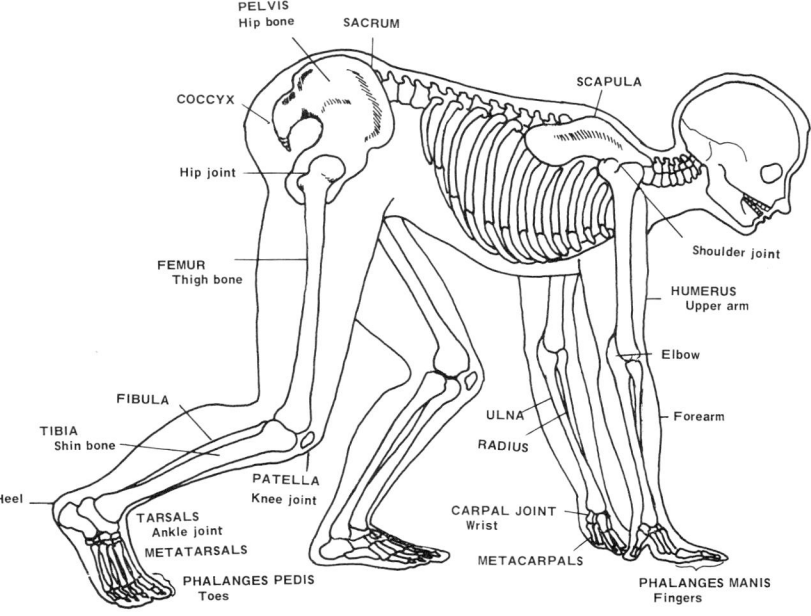

Evolution has changed the horse into a weight-carrying animal, chiefly by altering his legs from the hock and the knee down. He used to walk on four toes in front, and three in back, but now walks on a single toe in each foot. Though there is but a semblance of some of the original bones left in his legs, the scientific names remain, and horses and dogs still share the same principles of locomotion.

Function influences form. For example, here is a variety of dog developed through selective breeding to ferret out farm pests from underground. The elbows became set above the line of the brisket in order to free the legs for digging, while the dog's weight came to rest on his chest. The long and gradual upward slant of the lower rib cage helps him to slide more easily over rocks and roots—a handy arrangement in case there is need for speedy retreat.

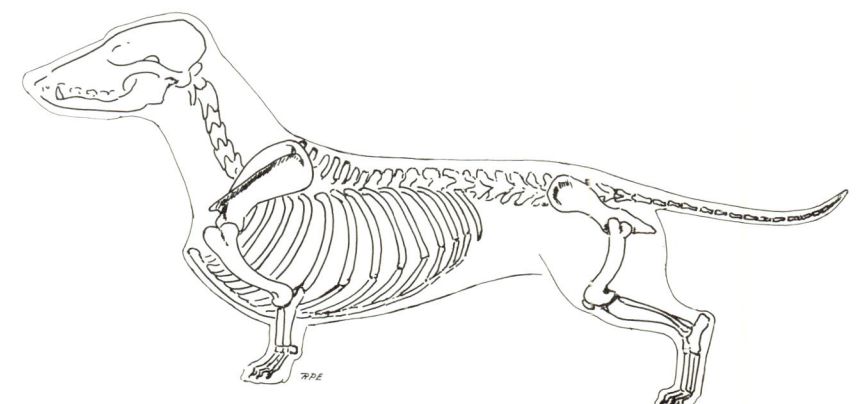

2.

The Natural Gaits . . .

Gait Patterns Defined

The Natural Gaits—

The term **gait** means pattern of footsteps at various rates of speed, each pattern distinguished by a particular rhythm and footfall. The *walk,* the *trot,* and the *gallop* are perhaps the most commonly recognized of the gaits, but *ambling, pacing,* and *cantering* are also normal ways in which many four-footed animals move.

The two gaits acceptable in the show ring are the walk and the trot. When a judge requests an exhibitor to "Gait your dog," he means simply that the dog be led (usually at the trot) across the ring and back, so that he may evaluate the dog's way of moving and how it relates to his conformation.

THE WALK seems so uncomplicated there is no need to analyze it other than to draw contrast with the faster gaits which cause the dog to rely on speed for balance and stability. At the walk, three legs are in support of the body at all times, each foot lifting from the ground one at a time in regular sequence. The pattern of footfall is right hind, right front, left hind, left front.

THE AMBLE is like a fast rocking walk with *an irregular four-beat cadence* in which the legs on either side move *almost*—but not quite—as a pair. This relaxed, easy movement is characteristic of a few large breeds, but all dogs amble now and then. Often seen as a transition movement between the walk and faster gaits, ambling should not be confused with pacing.

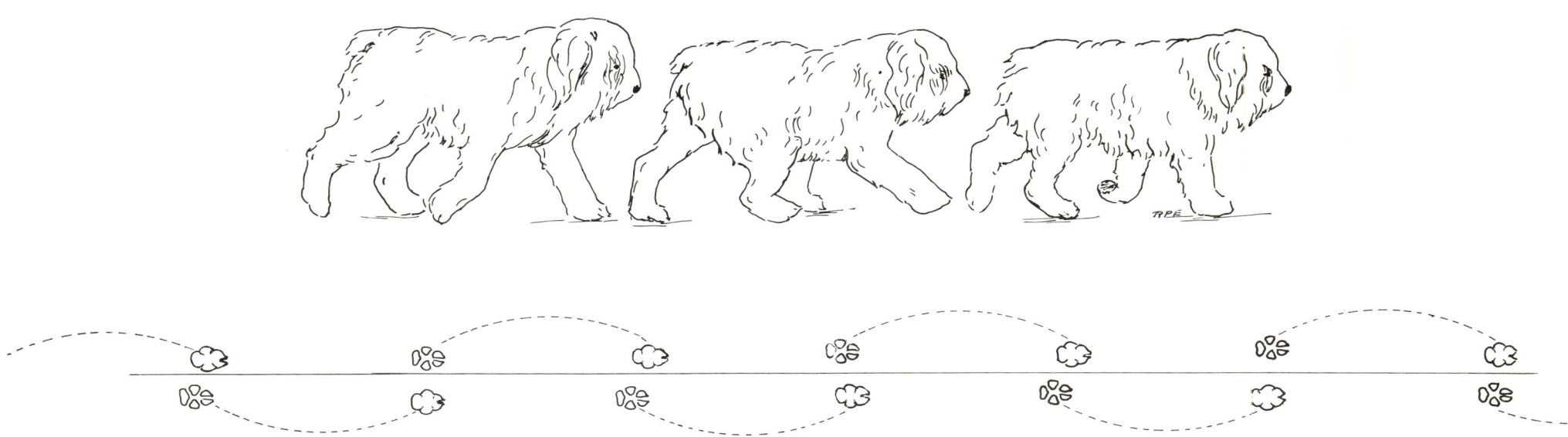

THE PACE is *a two-beat lateral gait,* in which the legs on each side move back and forth exactly as a pair, causing a rolling or rocking motion of the dog's body. Structure and proportion have a direct influence on a dog's inclination to pace. This gait is characteristic of a few large breeds, but it is frowned upon in the show ring. The action is sometimes called "side-wheeling".

Early pacing horses, at first not fully appreciated for their racing potential, were dubbed "side-wheelers", a term from steamboat terminology. The long legs and great speed of modern pacers minimizes body roll.

THE TROT is a rhythmic two-beat diagonal gait in which the feet at diagonally opposite ends of the body strike the ground together, i.e. right hind with left front and left hind with right front. Because only two feet are on the ground at a time, the dog must rely on forward momentum for balance. At a normal trot, in a dog of these proportions, the imprint of the hind feet tends to cover the tracks left by the front.

Diagonal leg action distinguishes trotters from pacers among harness horses.

HACKNEY GAITING is a variation of the trot, distinguished by *high flashy action* in the front and rear legs. To be correct, the topline should remain as level as possible as the dog moves, all the action being in the exaggerated flexing of the joints. This gait is characteristic of a few small breeds.

The term derives from hackney horses which are bred specifically for this type of action.

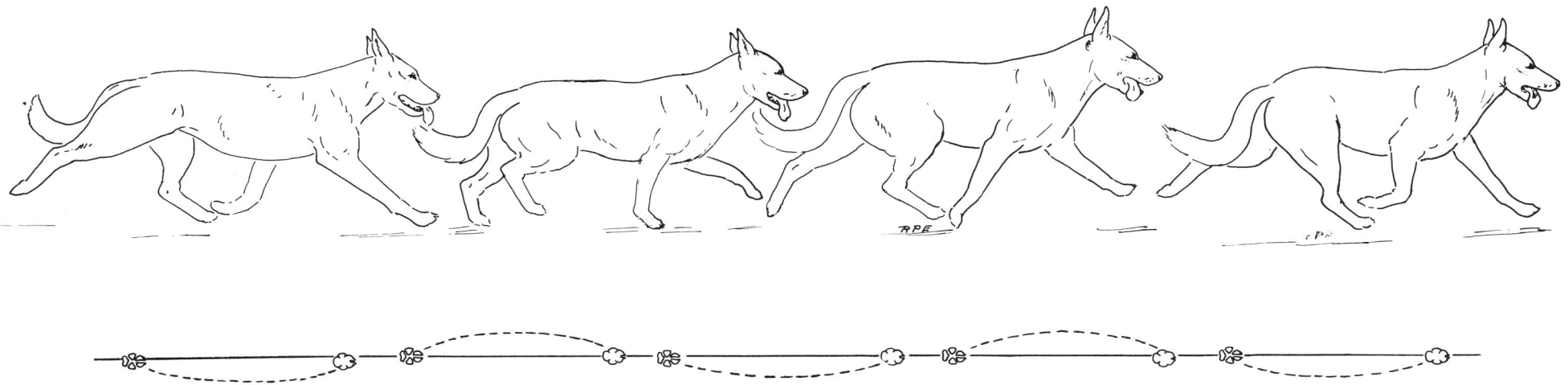

THE SUSPENSION or FLYING TROT, is a *fast gait* in which all four feet are off the ground for a brief second during each half stride. Because of the long reach, the oncoming hind feet step beyond the imprint left by the front. Coordination and good foot timing are of great importance to avoid interference or striking.

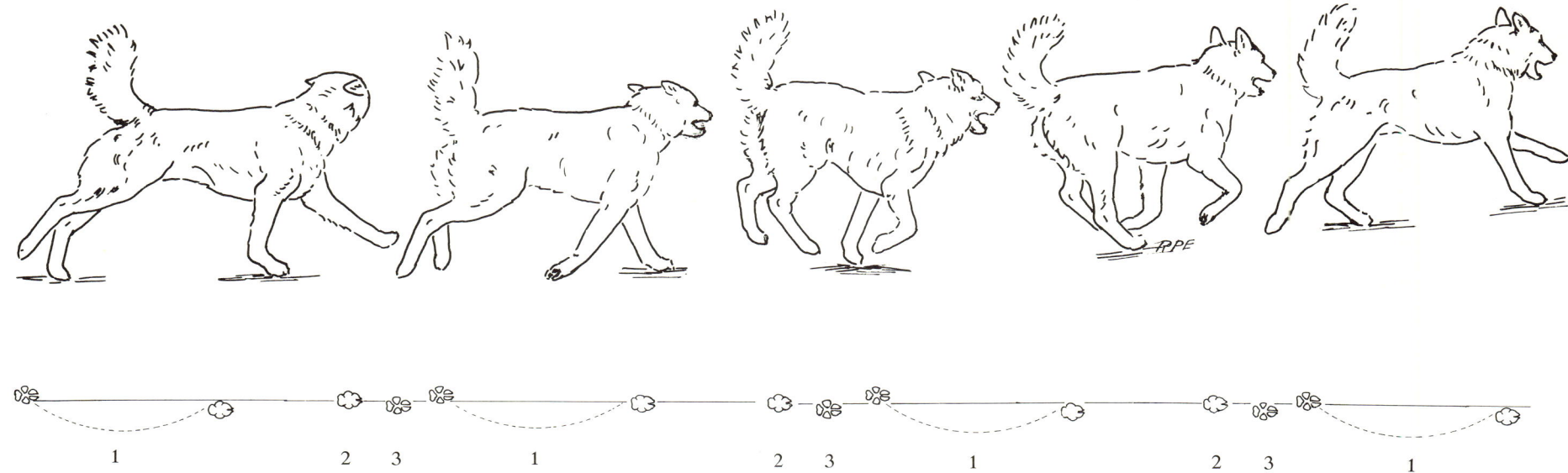

Paws connected with dotted line move as a pair.

THE CANTER, a gait slower than the gallop and not as tiring, *has three beats to each stride*—two legs moving separately and two as a diagonal pair. When the dog "leads" with the left front foot (as in this illustration), the right front moves simultaneously with the left rear. Cantering is sometimes referred to as the "collected gallop" or the "lope", but such references are to rate of speed rather than pattern of footfall, as they differ from the canter in this last respect.

Sound sled dogs cover the miles at a steady "lope".

THE GALLOP, fastest of the gaits, has a *four-beat rhythm,* and often an extra period of suspension during which the body is propelled through the air with all four feet off the ground. I have seen no better description of the gallop than the following, written by the famous canine authority, "Stonehenge":*

> Perfection of the gallop depends upon the power of extending the shoulders and forelegs as far as possible, as well as bringing the hind legs rapidly forward to give the propulsive stroke. If the hindquarters are good and well-brought into action, while the shoulders do not thrust the forelegs well forward, the action is laboured and slow. On the contrary, if the shoulders do their duty, but the hind legs are not brought well forward, or do not thrust the body onwards with sufficient force, the action may be elegant, but it is not powerful and rapid. For these purposes, therefore, we require good shoulders, good thighs, a good back, and good legs, and, lastly, for lodging the lungs and heart, whose actions are essential for the maintenance of speed, a well-formed and capacious chest.

* "Stonehenge": *The Dogs of the British Islands,* Second Edition, London 1872, p. 180.

A combination of sound conformation, good body balance, and the spirit to win, pay off as galloping race hounds near the finish line.

3.

Good Performance Is the Test of Good Structure

Dogs that are built well can stand long days of hard work.

A good working dog has limbs that extend freely...

and balance of body for trotting long hours without tiring.

Strong hindquarters provide strength for quick bursts of speed . . .

and thrust for leaping.

Good proportion and strong loins lend suppleness to the back . . .

as strong pasterns and thick pads help reduce the shock of sudden impact.

Well-built hindquarters and good shoulders provide stamina for trailing with nose to the ground.

This type of farm dog will drive a herd of cows and, because of its low sturdy frame, can easily dodge kicking heels.

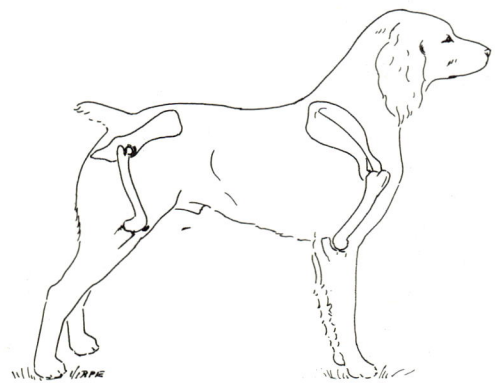

Good structure means symmetry of proportion, which provides a smooth, effortless gait, with all parts moving in harmonious rhythm.

A strong, even gait is desirable in all breeds . . .

no matter the size . . .   the shape . . .   or purpose.

4.

Angulation and Balance . . .

Foundation of Structure and Movement

The Importance of Angulation

Essential to the appearance and qualities of endurance in all dogs are the structural features which govern balance and the ability to move freely—called "angulation". Good angulation contributes to long, effortless stride and smooth action. Poor angulation tends to shorten stride and make a dog's action stilted or choppy.

Angulation has to do with the size of the angles at certain joints. Those influencing structure and gait most are the shoulder and hip joints, formed by the largest, strongest bones in the dog's body. These joints act as open-and-shut hinges as the humerus and femur swing the limbs forward and back. The more normal the angulation, the longer the arc of swing, and therefore, the freer the action. Hips consist of ball and socket construction, and for this reason have greater rotating facility than other joints, but correct angulation is still necessary for best performance.

There are generally ideal measurements for every form or figure, and authorities on canine anatomy have been no exception in arriving at standards of perfection for shoulder and hip angulation in dogs. Stated simply, the ideal shoulder blade should slant at 45 degrees to the ground, forming an approximate right angle with the humerus at the shoulder joint. The pelvis should have a 30-degree slant, forming a right angle with the femur at the hip socket. Sound reasoning supports these measurements, even though variations occur in fronts and rears due to type and purpose. There are marked differences among breeds in width and depth of chest, for example, as well as in length and character of the upper arm. However, such differences should not be accepted at the sacrifice of proper slant to the shoulder blade. As a friend of mine once said, "The shoulder should have good layback no matter what hangs from it."

The degree of angulation at the hip joint, together with the relative length of the leg bones, influences the bend of stifle and hock. These joints play a vital role in providing strength and drive to the hindquarters.

Good angulation facilitates a long stride. Balance facilitates good foot-timing. Joints that control movement should flex easily and smoothly, providing strong thrust from the rear limbs, and spring and resilience in the forehand to absorb constant impact with the ground. The swing and reach of the forelegs should coordinate with the action of the rear so that there will be no over-stepping or interfering. As a general rule, the feet should move rather close to the ground so as to avoid excessive bending of the joints, which can be inefficient and tiring.

Poor angulation shortens stride because the bones meeting at the shoulder joint and the hip are steeply set, and form joints with wide open angles. This limits swing of the upper arm and the thigh bone, restricting reach of the forelegs and drive from the rear. Dogs so constructed must take shorter steps—and more of them—to get where they are going, and their action is bouncing rather than smooth. The dog above is too straight, both front and rear; but in spite of this fault, and a short stilted gait, his body appears to be in balance.

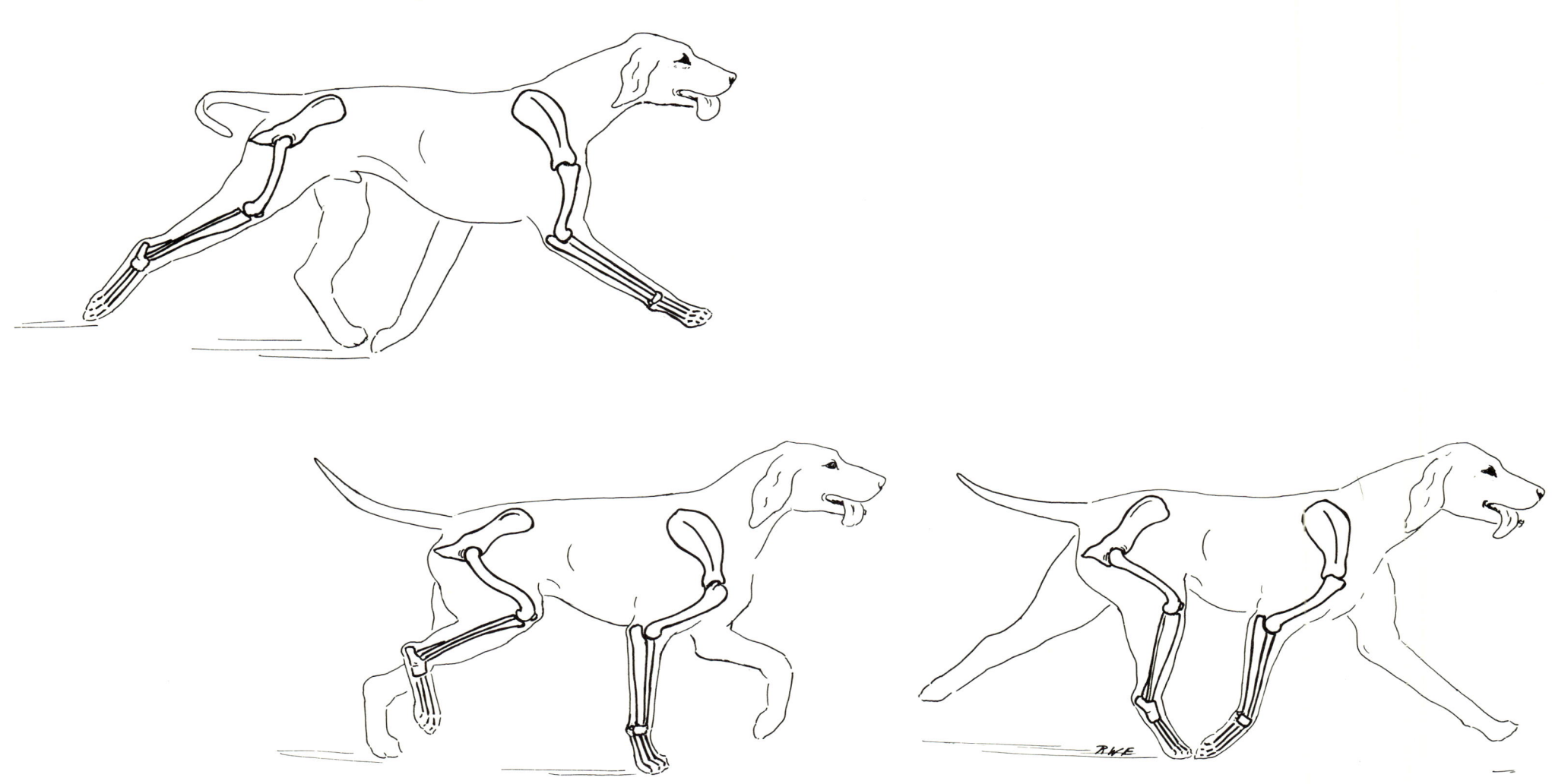

"Practically the whole propelling force of the hind limb is dependent on the ability of the dog to straighten the leg from the state of angulation to complete extension, as forcibly and as rapidly as may be required. This is dependent entirely upon the muscle power of a well-developed second thigh."
—Smythe: *Conformation of the Dog*.

"Sickle hocks" (*fault*)

Contrasting sharply with the suppleness of the dog on the opposite page is this dog with "sickle hocks." The term is derived from the sickle, a farm tool with a rigid angle where the handle meets the blade. Sickle-hocked action is stiff and shuffling, with almost no use of the hock joint to help in forward propulsion. A sickle-hocked dog usually stands with his pasterns angled slightly forward, never standing "well up on his hocks." In this particular dog, the front quarters are very straight, and because of almost no push from the rear, most of his energy is spent bobbing up and down.

The Value of Balance

Balance depends not only on the proportion of head to neck, depth of chest to length of legs, and overall length of body to height, but also on a front end that matches the rear. In other words, when a dog is standing naturally, the angulation at the shoulder and hip joints should be approximately equal, in order to provide the same amount of reach in the forelegs as in the rear. (See page 45).

A dog is not in balance if the shoulder and upper arm are steeply set and the hindquarters are well-angulated, because he will have a short stride in front and a long stride in the rear. Conversely, he is not in balance if the front is well-angulated but the hindquarters are steep, because this will mean good reach in front but a shorter stride in the rear—and the front quarters will overwork. It is possible for a dog that is equally steep fore and aft to be in balance—and he may be better off than one that lacks balance—but he will not have the quality of movement that is achieved when balance is combined with good angulation. (See page 55, sequence A).

Lack of structural balance is the reason for much incorrect gaiting. A few illustrations of this point may be seen on the next five pages.

OVERREACHING at the trot is a common fault, caused by more angulation and drive from behind than in front, so that the rear feet are forced to step to one side of the forefeet to avoid interfering or clipping. This is one of the many forms of poor foot-timing, but it must not be confused with the natural overreach in the suspension trot, or in the canter or gallop.

HACKNEY ACTION *as a fault* is caused by more angulation and drive from behind than in front, but instead of overreaching the dog resorts to a quick, extra high action of the forelegs in order to keep the paws out of the way of the oncoming back feet. The action is bouncy rather than smooth, as evidenced by the tips of this little dog's ears, which flip up and down with each step. Cute as it may appear to ringside spectators, hackneying is a waste of energy and very tiring. It should not be confused with the normal hackney action characteristic of a few small breeds whose high action is confined to leg joints and achieved only through proper angulation.

"Padding" and "Running Downhill" (*faults*)

"PADDING" is a compensating action to offset constant concussion when a straight front is subjected to overdrive, or too much thrust, from the rear. The front feet flip upward in a split-second delaying action to better coordinate stride of the forelimbs with the longer stride from behind. This tends to keep the front feet from slamming into the ground and thus helps to lessen the pounding through steeply-set pasterns and shoulder bones. The action is almost too quick for the eye to follow, as the front feet land carefully, far back on the heels, with the thickest part of the pads acting as buffers against impact with the ground. Strain on the front quarters is accentuated when a dog is lower at the withers than in the hindquarters, as illustrated here. Such structure gives him the appearance of "running downhill."

"Running Downhill" (*fault*)

Youth has its problems. Puppies often develop faster in the rear end than in the front, which gives them the appearance of running downhill even though they are on level ground. Long dogs with short legs never have to cope with the inconvenience of rear feet overstepping the front, but lack of balance still impairs symmetry and overall appearance.

"Pounding" (*fault*)

"POUNDING" is another gaiting fault which results from the dog's stride being shorter in front than in the rear. The forefeet strike the ground before the rear stride is expended. If a dog with this fault does nothing to spare himself, such as "padding", "hackneying" or pacing, the thrust from the hindquarters causes the front feet to hit the ground hard, as happens when a person is pushed suddenly and is forced to take a quick step before his joints can properly "give" to cushion the impact. In the dog, such impact has a pile-driving effect through pasterns and shoulder bones, causing abrupt choppy action at the withers. Constant "pounding" tends to bruise joint cartilage, and may eventually cause the dog to "break down in front."

"Broken Pasterns" and "Overreaching" (*faults*)

A straight front with low withers forces this dog to land heavily with each step. Constant pounding has weakened ligaments and tendons in the pasterns to the point where they bend far too much as the dog's weight passes over the front quarters. Also called "down at the pasterns".

How Angulation Affects Muscle Structure

In the preceding pages, angulation has been discussed as it relates to length of stride and to balance. Another important consideration is how it affects muscle structure.

Diagrams on the opposite page show three concepts each of two different dogs: "A" with good angulation and "B" with poor angulation.

Dog "A" illustrates how good angulation gives wider spread to the muscles, due to the fact that the shoulder bones and the pelvis are properly slanted. This slant seems to provide more area for muscle attachment and lends strength and substance to the dog's appearance. Good angulation also goes hand-in-hand with a strong middle piece, and with a rib cage that extends well back.

Correct placement of the scapula, called "good shoulder layback", contributes to dog "A's" reach of neck and good head carriage, and gives the neckline a pleasing transition into the withers and topline. In conformation terms, this is referred to as a "neck well-set-on" or "setting well into the shoulders."

Dog "B's" upright structure in both front and rear quarters illustrates how poor angulation tends to reduce the size and slant of the bones and affects the area of muscle attachment. In this type of dog, these bones are usually narrower, with the muscles relatively poorly developed, and it may be said the dog "lacks substance." In addition, steep shoulders detract from the dog's overall appearance because the neckline joins the withers abruptly and tends to make the neck look short.

Dotted lines in these two studies call attention to differences in width across front and rear quarters, and show at a glance that the dog with greater width has better angulation. Correct positioning of the shoulder and pelvis always lends breadth to the quarters (viewed in profile), from shoulder joint to a line dropped just behind the blade, and from the forward edge of the pelvis to the buttocks. It is such structure that clues us in to the better movers, whatever the breed of dog, for the principles and advantages of good angulation are the same for all.

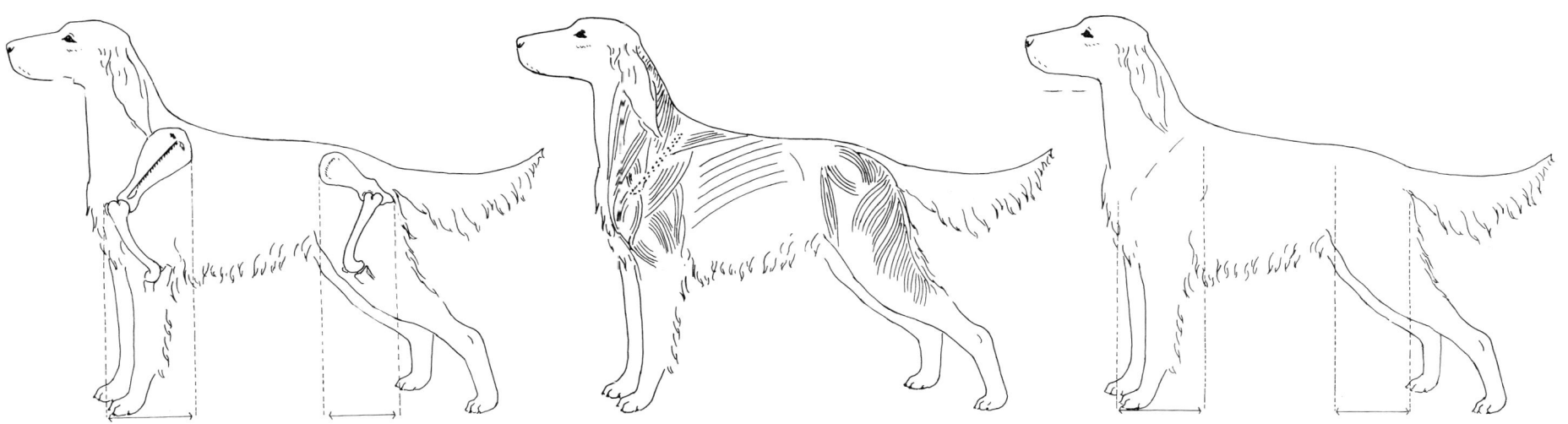

DOG "A"—Illustrating how good angulation provides the foundation for good muscle structure, lending breadth to the front and rear quarters and substance to the overall picture.

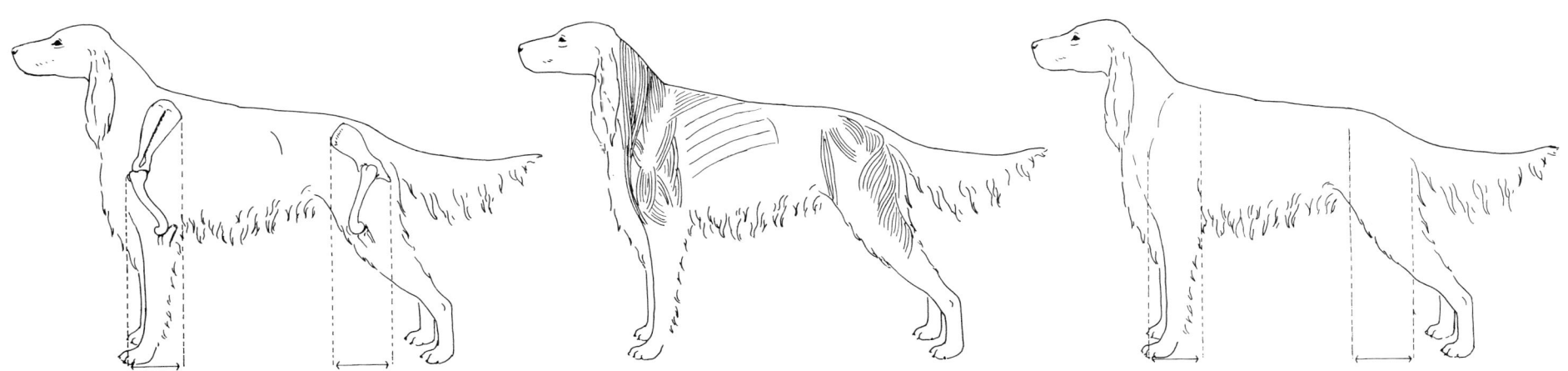

DOG "B"—Illustrating how poor angulation limits the foundation for muscle structure, narrowing the width across front and rear quarters, and giving the appearance of less substance.

More Hints on Determining Shoulder Layback

Many of us have difficulty judging front angulation because the bony structure in a dog's forequarters is not as prominent as it is in the rear. Unlike the line of the croup or the bend of the stifle and the hock, the bones forming the shoulder joint are obscured by heavy muscle or coat, so that often the exact position of the shoulder blade is not easy to determine—particularly in a class where the majority of the dogs are of mediocre quality. Contrasts in good and poor are not always as obvious as in these illustrations, but a few hints on what to look or feel for may prove helpful in quick side-view appraisals.

A first clue, as previously discussed, is to observe the width across the front quarters from forechest to just behind the shoulder blade, preferably when the dog is standing naturally.

A second and most telling clue is the point where the line of the neck joins the withers. This point, indicated by a slight dip in the dog's outline, falls just in front of the scapula at the start of the withers (see diagram on opposite page). Its location depends entirely on the set of the blade itself.

A third clue may be the slope of the pastern. Strong, moderately sloping pasterns almost invariably keep company with fair or good fronts because they are part of the bone assembly which receives and cushions impact from the ground. A pastern joint with a slight bend has spring and resilience. Pasterns which are upright take impact with the ground "head-on." Extreme cases of steep pasterns cause knuckling at the carpal joints, known as "over-at-the-knees." On the other hand, weak pasterns, called "down at the pasterns" or "broken pasterns," can be deceptive because they slope *too* much, regardless of the bone assembly above.

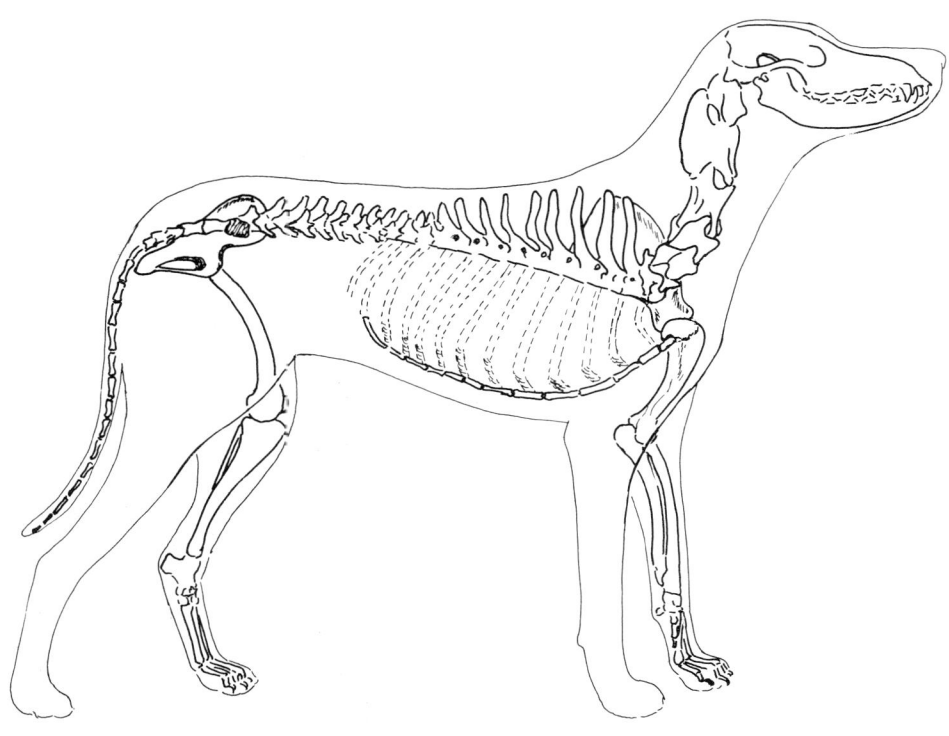

*From a drawing by Ernest W. Beck,
THE CANINE, Fromm Laboratories*

Cross section of a dog's skeleton, showing in general the position of the left shoulder blade against the long spinal vertebrae. Since the dog is not a tree-climbing animal, he has no collar bone, which means that the blade is attached to the spine and the ribs only by muscle. The pelvis, on the other hand, is firmly fixed to the spinal column at the sacrum and its movement is limited mainly to whatever suppleness there may be in the lumbar vertebrae which support the loin.

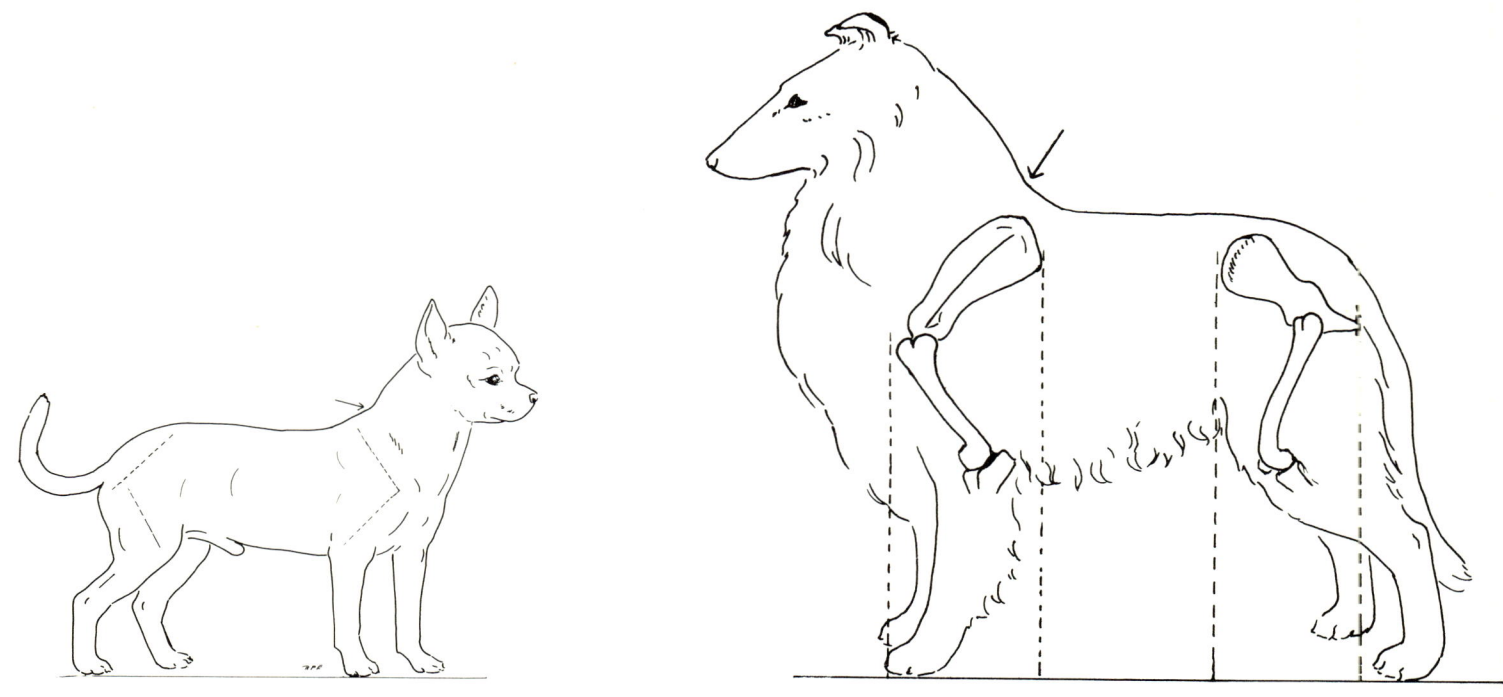

Two illustrations of what is meant by the expression "neck well-set-on"—good necklines merging gradually with strong withers, forming a pleasing transition into toplines. Arrows point to where the neck meets the withers just in front of the top of the shoulder blade, a point that usually can be detected on any dog if you know what to look for.

FLAT WITHERS(*fault*) are the result of short, upright shoulder blades which make for a neckline that unattractively joins the withers abruptly. Longhaired dogs are sometimes groomed to disguise faulty fronts, but true lay of the shoulder can be determined by feeling for it. Horsemen who know structure avoid animals with flat withers, not only because upright shoulders mean a hard pounding ride, but also because flat withers let the saddle slide forward.

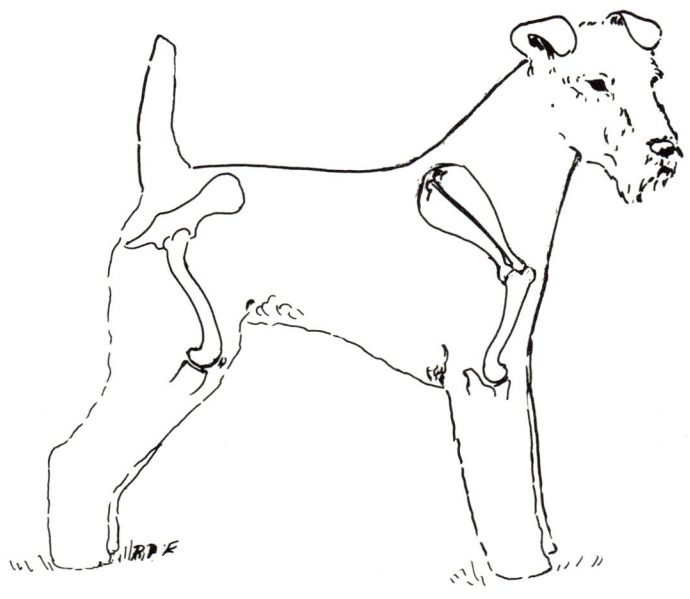

A good neckline above an obliquely-set shoulder, combined with correct angulation in the rear, illustrates the old expression: "Built like a cleverly made hunter—short in the back, but standing over a lot of ground."

A short neckline joining flat withers above steeply-set shoulders tends to give undesirable length to the back, particularly when combined with a steeply-set rear.

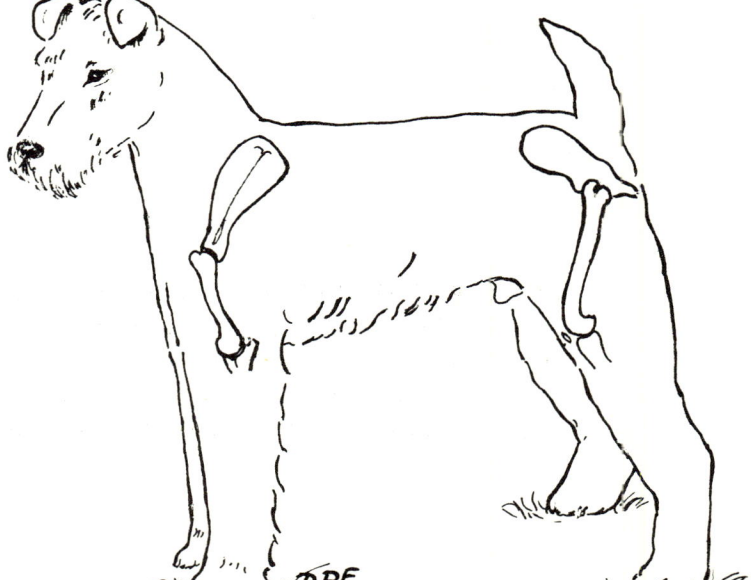

5.

Heads and Tails . . .

and A Few Other Views

Generally Speaking—

Semantics and Optical Illusion Cause Confusion

A FEW terms cause considerable misunderstanding about front and rear action, simply because they are used without clear definition. Expressions such as *parallel, standing straight, moving straight, inclining inward, moving close, toeing in, moving on the same plane, parallel tracks, parallel hocks, single tracking,* and others, not only confuse newcomers, but now and then cause lively discussion among some who have been in the dog game for many years.

The unfortunate aspect of this problem of semantics is that it occasionally permits one to condone certain faulty action, or casts a shadow on action that is correct. It is also a possible reason for faults being perpetuated by innocent parties who try to breed dogs to move in a way never intended by nature. There is a common fallacy, for example, that trotting dogs should move with their legs parallel with each other. Surely such thinking must be influenced by optical illusion, for slow motion photography has long since shown that normal leg movement inclines slightly inward, dependent—of course—on the type of dog and his rate of travel. Misunderstanding of this principle has brought the unjust criticism of "moving too close" on many a dog that actually is moving well. Parallel movement is contrary to nature's laws of balance and motion. Breeders who try to achieve it must sacrifice angulation, and handlers who try to achieve it must resort to tight leads, substituting stilted short action for good natural reach.

The sequence sketches that follow illustrate variations in gaiting as dogs come and go from the viewer, and should help to clarify more of the common faults that often puzzle us.

Legs "Not Moving on the Same Plane" (*fault*)

When the hind feet do not follow the tracks made by the front feet, the legs are not inclining inward to the same extent and the action is faulty. Many gaiting faults fall under this category.

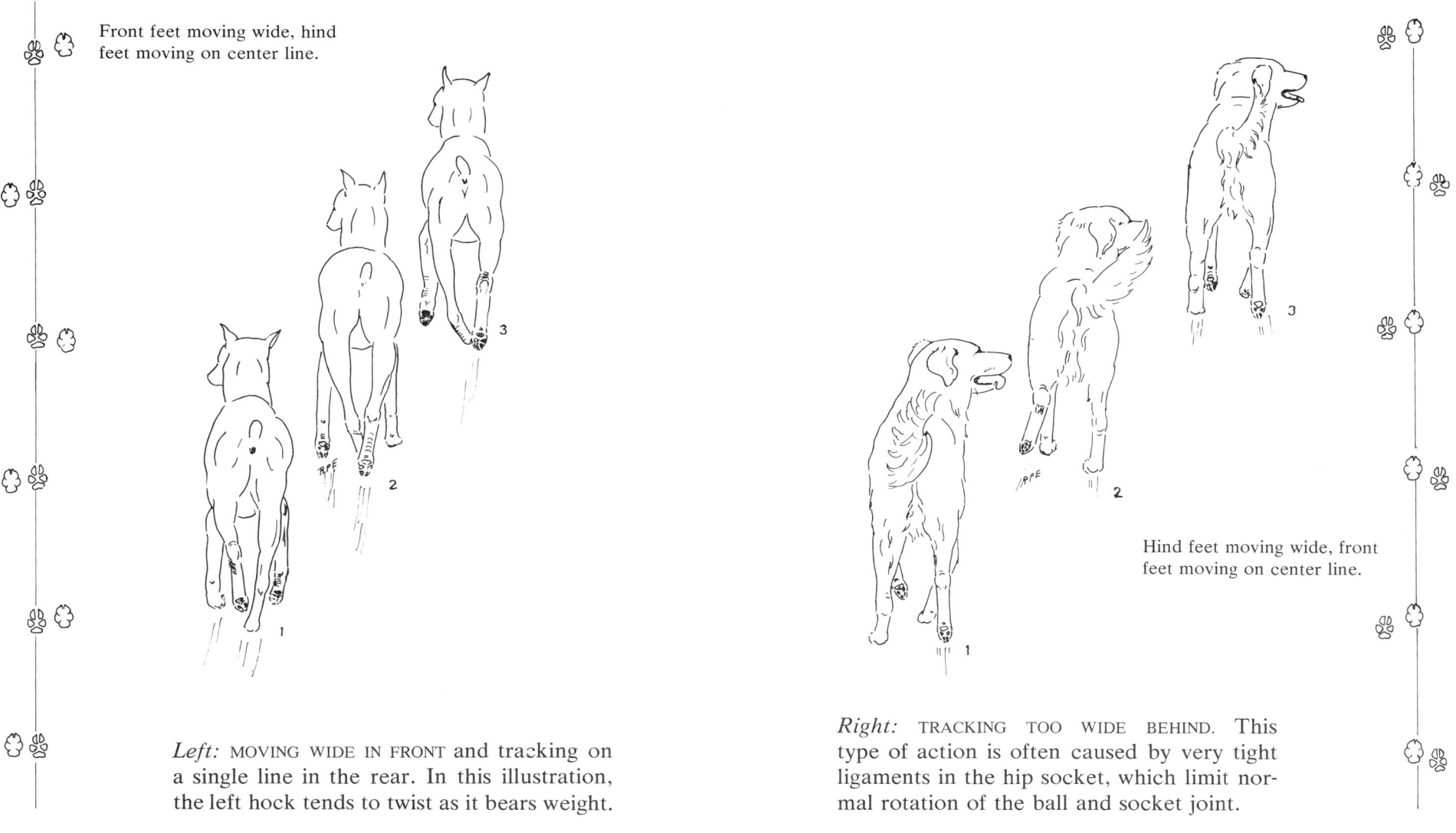

Front feet moving wide, hind feet moving on center line.

Hind feet moving wide, front feet moving on center line.

Left: MOVING WIDE IN FRONT and tracking on a single line in the rear. In this illustration, the left hock tends to twist as it bears weight.

Right: TRACKING TOO WIDE BEHIND. This type of action is often caused by very tight ligaments in the hip socket, which limit normal rotation of the ball and socket joint.

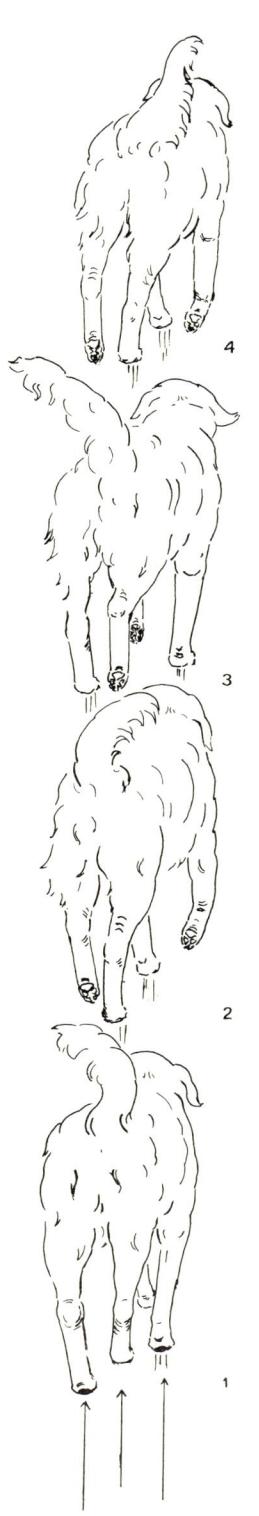

"Crabbing" (*fault*)

"Crabbing" is a common fault, in which the dog moves with his body at an angle to the line of travel. The action is frequently due to more angulation in the rear than in the front, in combination with a short, stiff back. When a dog takes longer steps with his hind legs than with his forelimbs, he can avoid striking or interfering by trotting with his hindquarters swung to one side. However, because the legs do not "move on the same plane", the gait is awkward and inefficient.

The term "crabbing" originates with the seacrab, which crawls forward in sidewise fashion. The fault is also occasionally referred to as "yawing," or as "side-winding." Careless handling or lack of leash training often causes dogs that normally would move straight to "crab."

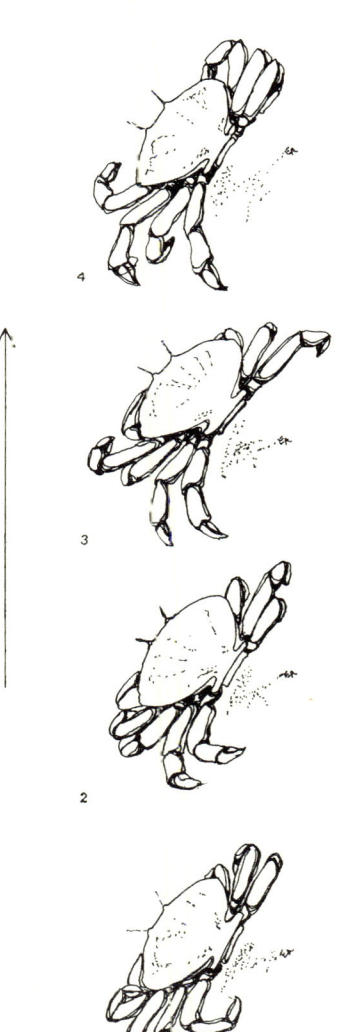

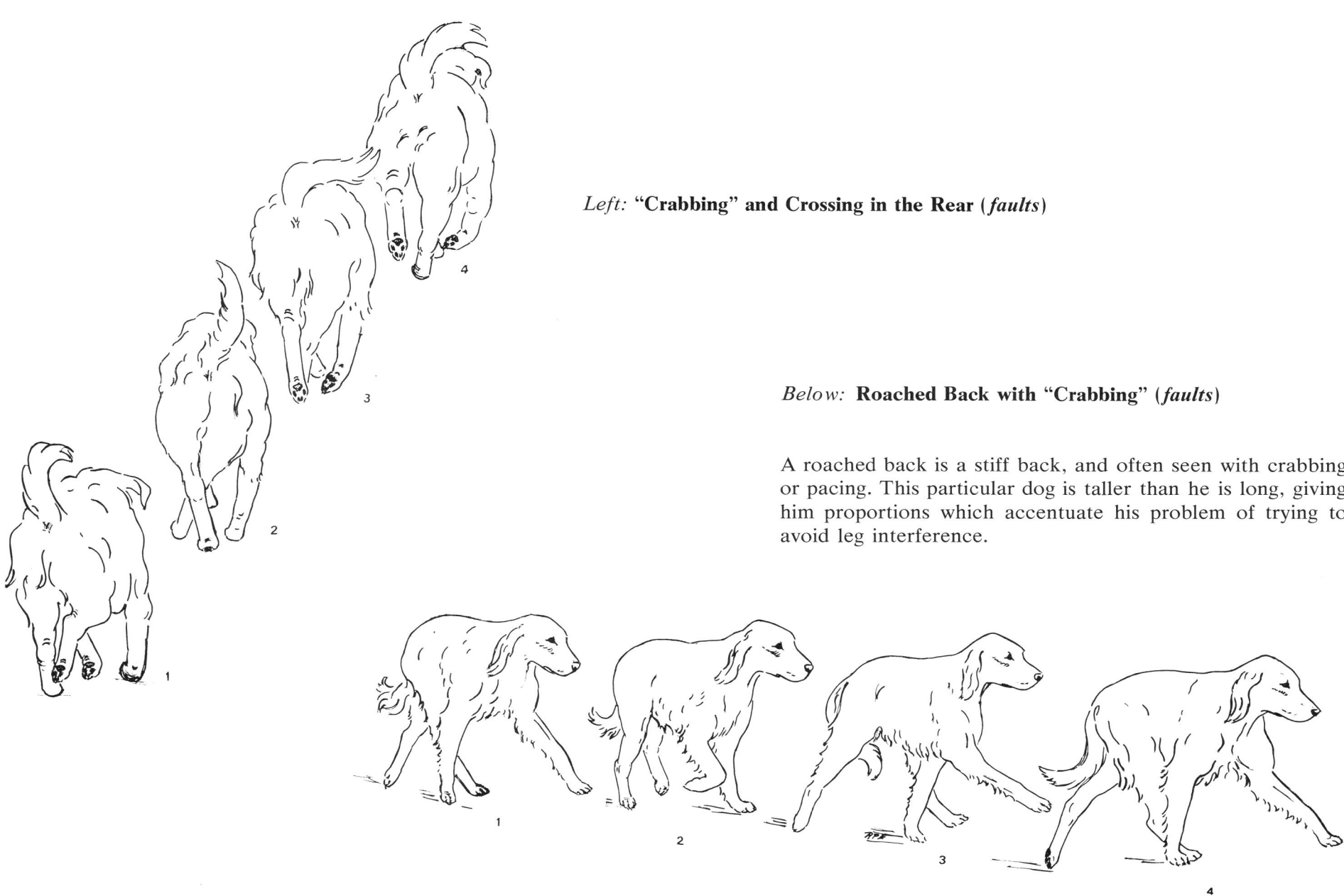

Left: **"Crabbing" and Crossing in the Rear** (*faults*)

Below: **Roached Back with "Crabbing"** (*faults*)

A roached back is a stiff back, and often seen with crabbing or pacing. This particular dog is taller than he is long, giving him proportions which accentuate his problem of trying to avoid leg interference.

"Weaving" or "Knitting and Purling" (*fault*)

Well nicknamed is this unsound action, which starts with twisting elbows, and ends with crisscrossing pasterns and toeing out.

"Moving Close" and "Stifles Out" (*faults*)

When the hocks turn in, and the pasterns drop straight to the ground and move parallel to one another, the dog is "moving close" in the rear. In some cases, as in this illustration, the stifle is also thrown out of line. Action of this sort places severe strain on ligaments and muscles.

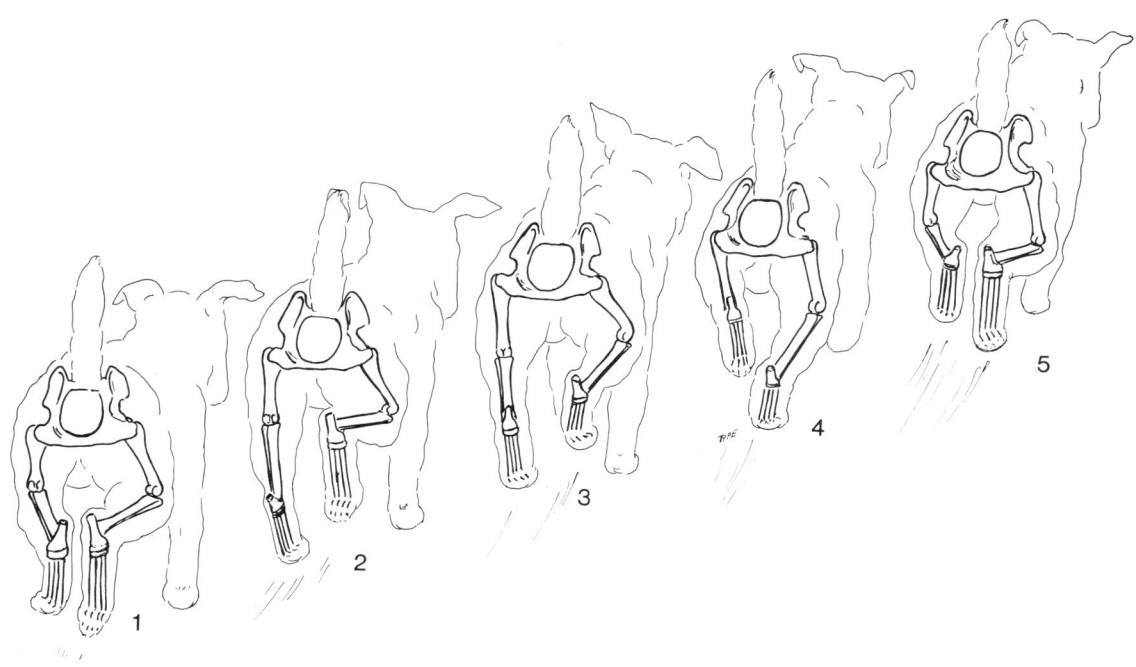

"Moving Close" and "Brushing" (*faults*)

Left: Parallel pasterns are sometimes so close that the legs "brush" in passing.

Right: Interfering and Crossing (*faults*)

"Cowhocks" (*fault*)

Cows often stand with their hocks turned in, and their stifles turned out, to accommodate large udders more comfortably. "Cowhocks" in dogs seriously weaken rear thrust.

This dog is not only cowhocked, but is also crossing his legs in front—a fault no doubt accentuated, because he is pulling to one side from his handler.

"Snatching Hocks" (*fault*)

This fault is indicated by a quick outward snatching of the hock as it passes the supporting leg and twists the rear pastern far in beneath the body. It is a compensating action to offset discomfort in the stifle joint. The action causes noticeable rocking in the rear quarters.

"Spread Hocks" (*fault*)

Hocks that turn out are called "spread hocks", "barrel hocks", "divergent hocks", or "hocking out". Like other faults, it shows up in varying degrees of severity. It always causes the feet to "toe in" (just the opposite from "cowhocks", which causes "toeing out").

Right: "Spread hocks", combined with "crossing in front".

"Twisting Hocks" (*fault*)

Also called "rubber hocks" or "weak hocks", this fault differs from "spread hocks" and "cowhocks" in that the joints twist both ways as they flex or bear weight.

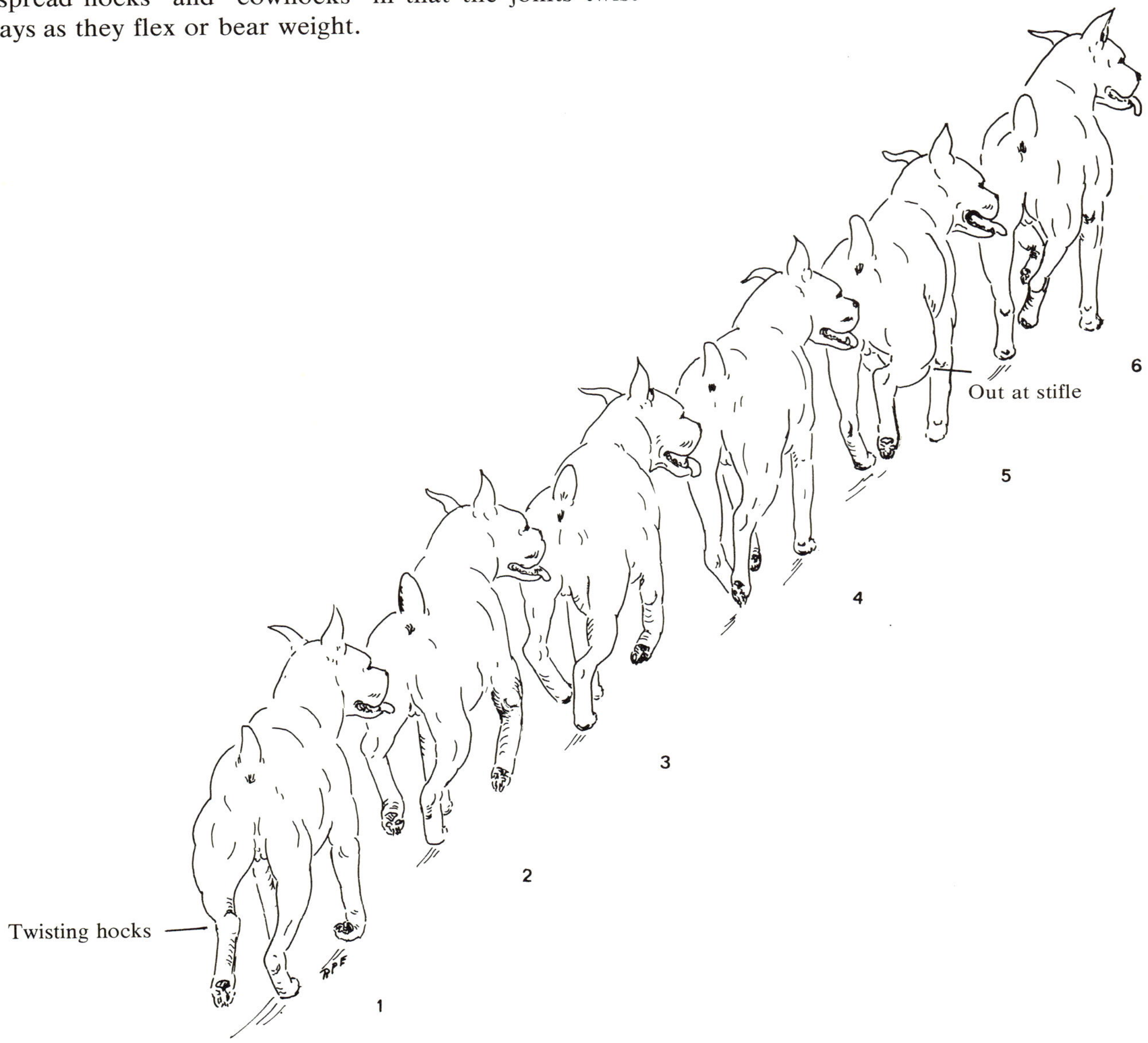

Out at stife

Twisting hocks

"Pitching" and "Crossing" (*faults*)

"Pitching" is characterized by severe rocking of the haunches as the rear legs swing forward in a wide arc, rather than flexing normally at the stifle and the hock. The action appears to be motivated in the croup, rather than through natural propulsion in the leg joints. The sway of the body is so pronounced that at times both front and rear feet cross the center line for balance.

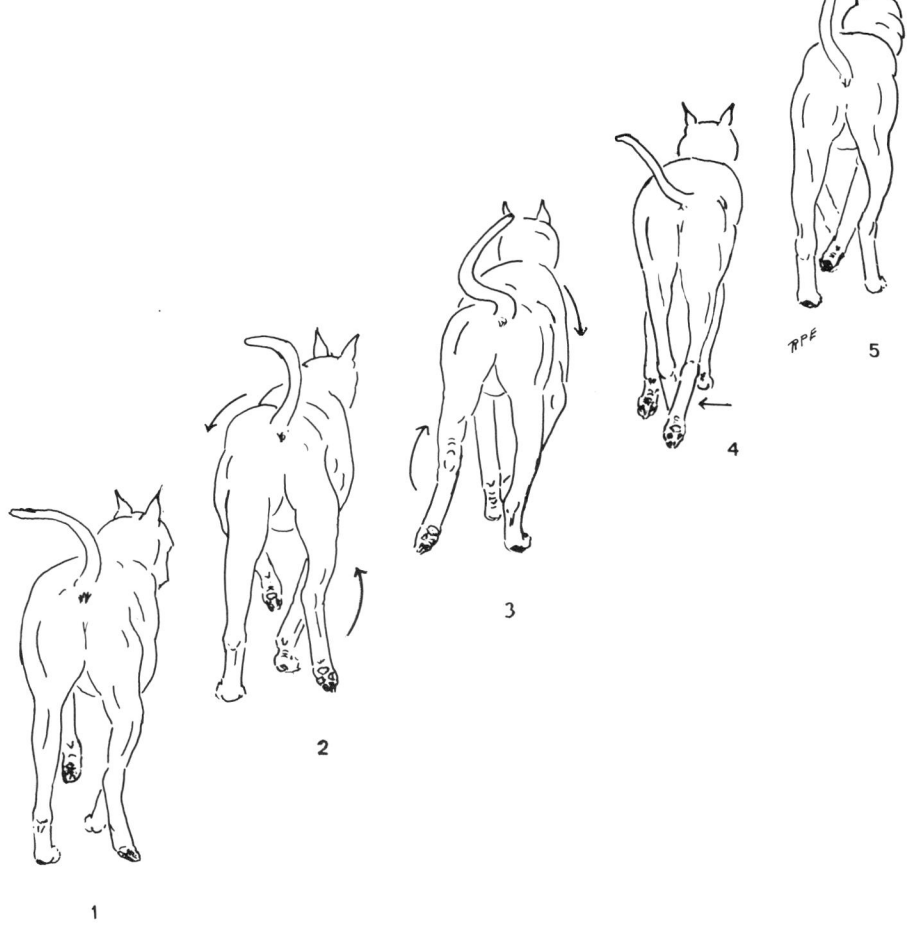

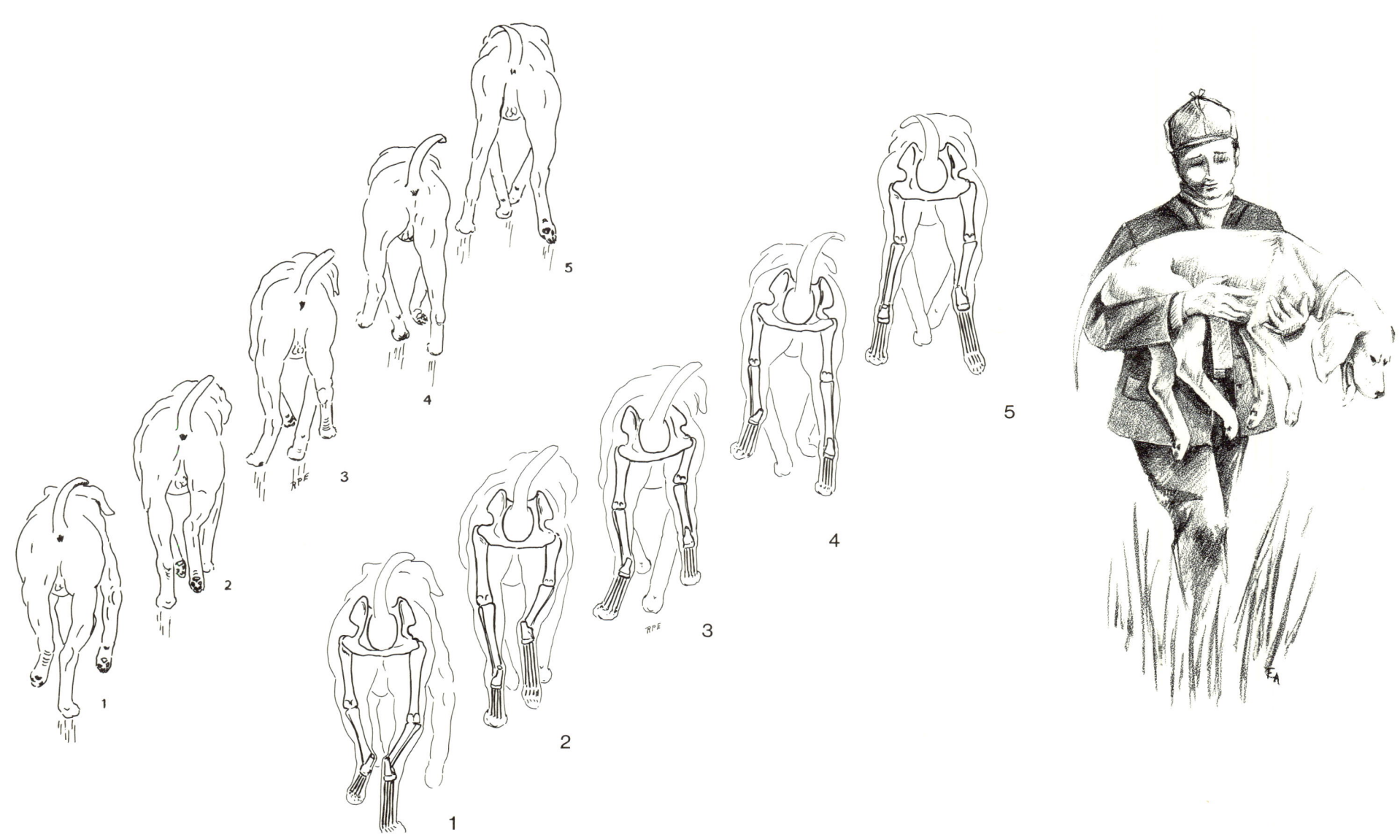

"Pitching" combined with "Cowhocks" (*faults*)

Twisting joints mean wear and tear on ligaments and muscles—more than sufficient reason for complete exhaustion after a day in the field.

Because of their structure, short-legged, broadly-built dogs move with some body roll, but those that move well minimize this tendency through the natural inclination of the legs toward a center line of balance beneath their bodies.

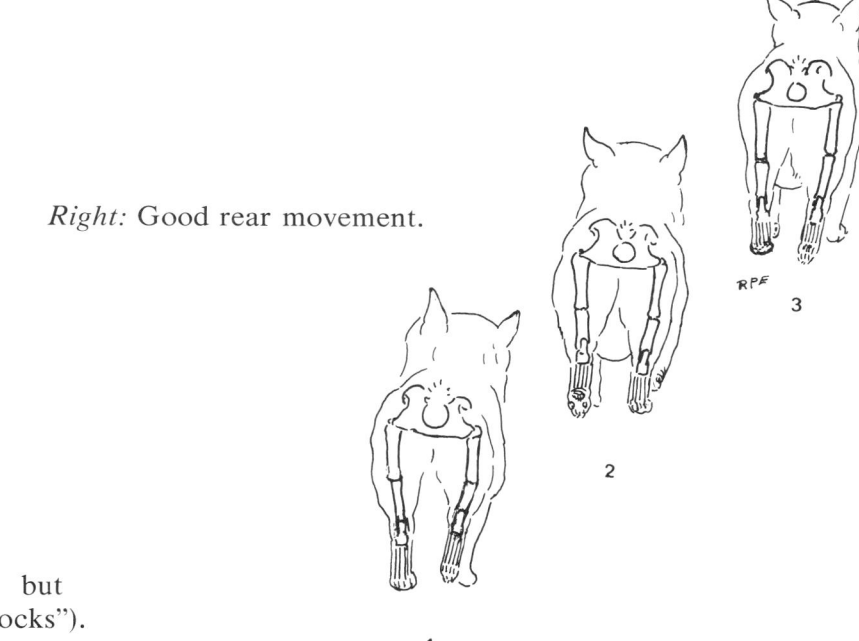

Right: Good rear movement.

Left: Moving well in front, but "toeing out" in the rear ("cowhocks").

Left: **"Toeing Out" or the "East-West Front"** (*fault*)
Arrows point to weak carpal joints, which bend inward, causing the feet to turn out.

Right: **"Moving Too Wide"** in front, **"Too Close"** in the rear, and **"Toeing In"**. (*faults*)

Championship Titles Do Not Guarantee Perfection

If you plan to raise dogs, study the pedigrees carefully. Most faults tend to be inherited, and serious defects which become deeply entrenched can imperil the soundness of breeding strains.

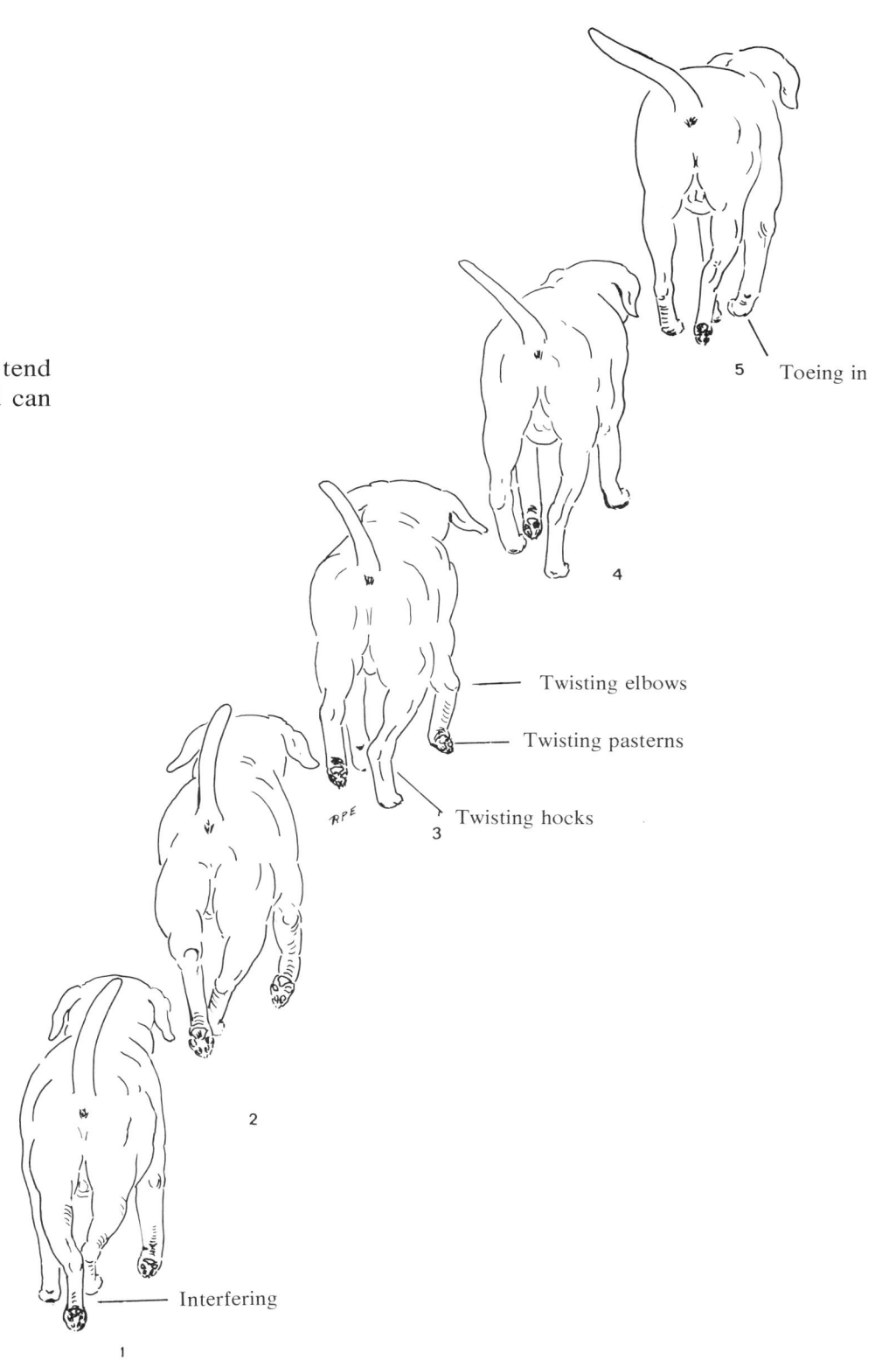

Elbows often cause trouble by "moving out". (fault)

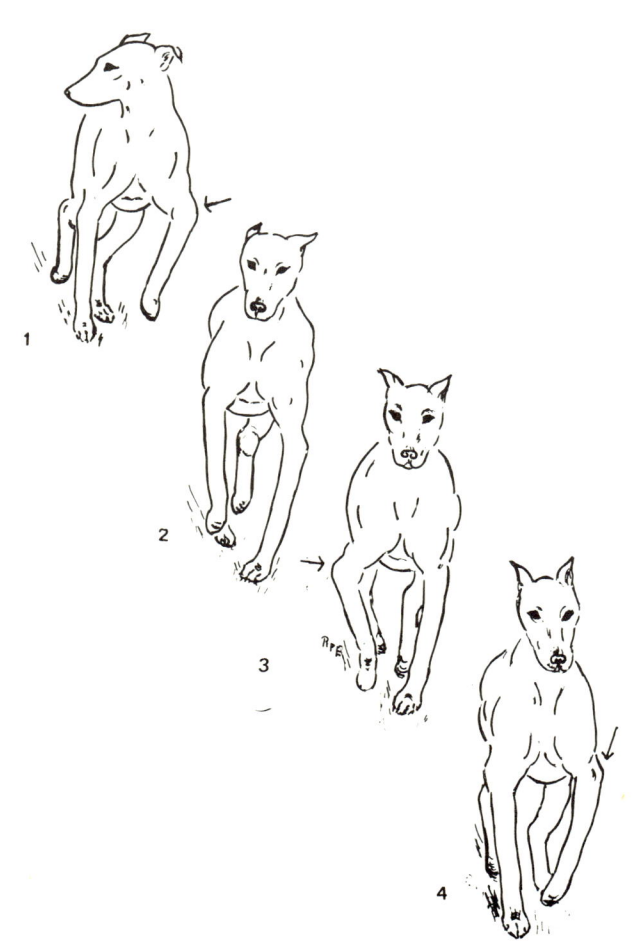

"Tied at the Elbows" or "Paddling" (fault)

is just the opposite sort of action from elbows moving out, and is generally considered a more serious defect because it so severely restricts front movement. Pinching in at the elbows, as well as at the shoulder joints, causes the front legs to swing forward on a stiff outward arc. Because of the wide footfall, the dog is said to travel "basewide", and the body rocks from side to side.

The term "paddling" derives from the swing and dip of the paddle as the canoeist keeps his canoe on course.

"Overreaching," Due to More Height than Length (*fault*)

Overreaching is a common fault in puppies as they develop through "leggy" stages when height at the withers may exceed length from buttocks to shoulder point by a fractional difference. Interesting action is illustrated here in that this young dog places his right hind foot first to the outside of the front leg, and then to the inside in the effort to avoid striking.

Pacing as a Result of "Square" Body Structure

Mature dogs that are "squarely" built, but tend to stand a bit lower at the withers than at the croup, often develop a natural tendency to avoid leg interference by pacing, rather than trotting. In the lateral action, the body tends to roll as the dog shifts his weight from side to side.

The dog in these illustrations is a natural pacer. In the top sequence, he is pacing easily. In the sequence below, he is trotting awkwardly because he is forced to "crab" to avoid leg interference. Pacing is frowned upon in the show ring, regardless of breed.

Pacing and Ambling as "Fatigue" Gaits

The sketch above was drawn from a photograph of exhausted sled dogs as they neared the finish line of a race, most of them pacing or ambling to rest muscles weary from trotting and cantering. Here the pace and amble are rightly referred to as "fatigue" gaits, because the dogs have switched to lateral movement to relieve strain.

Pacing to Avoid Interference (*fault*)

Generally speaking, dogs need a little more length of body than height at the withers, in order to be able to coordinate drive from the rear with reach in the front. A dog that is *too* short usually lacks angulation in one end or the other and often in both. Sometimes, if rear angulation is better he may become a habitual pacer to keep the hind feet from stepping on the front, as illustrated above.

Illustrated below is the same dog trotting awkwardly as the rear legs have to by-pass the front. This is an extreme example of poor foot timing.

Overreaching

Pacing Due to Injury or Roached Back (*fault*)

Sometimes pacing is the result of injury or strain in the loin area, or it can be due to too much arch in the back, which restricts action of the croup muscles. A dog will move in the way which is easiest for him, whether it be to alleviate pain, or because of habit resulting from poor conformation.

How Do We Look to Others?

If we plan to exhibit in dogs shows, we should give our dogs the advantage they deserve through careful handling. Good handling brings out the best in a dog. Poor handling can impair his overall appearance, and give the impression of faults that are not really there. Mirrors are a great help in checking your handling.

When the judge requests that you "gait your dog" in the show ring, the straight-on approach is important—but remember, it is the dog, not you, who is under judgment.

A Tight Lead Is Often Detrimental

Left: Swinging from the end of a tight lead causes this dog to "cross" in front.

Above: Side pull on the lead accentuates the dog's tendency to "cross".

Left: **"Winging"** is usually a natural fault where one or both front feet twist outward as the limbs swing forward, but here the fault is introduced artificially by too tight a lead.

Winging

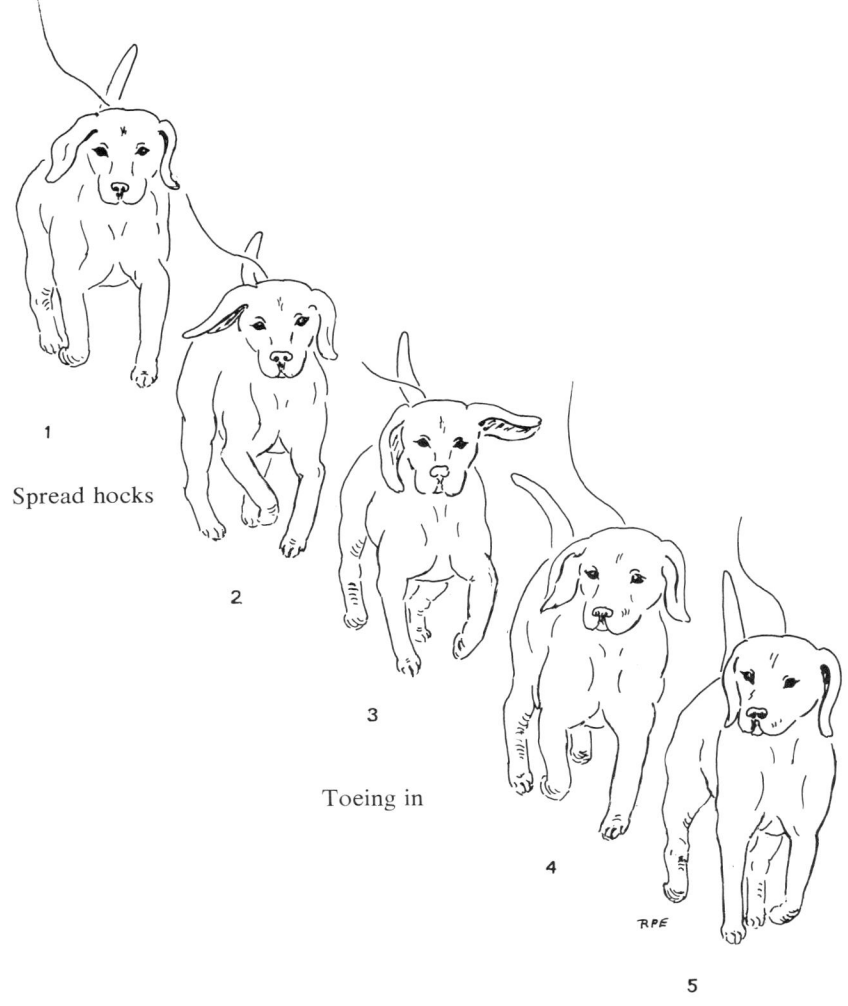

Spread hocks

Toeing in

Right: At the judge's request, "Loose lead, please," the same dog trots freely and exhibits his natural inclination to **"move wide in the hocks," "out at the elbows,"** and **"toe in"**.

Conclusion

At risk of being considered a "fault finder", the author may appear to have dwelt rather heavily on what makes a dog move incorrectly and not have stressed enough the features that make him move well. Unfortunately, faults tend to linger in one's impression, and too often override the total perspective. Such an imbalance was not our intent, but if our emphasis has stirred awareness of a few structural pitfalls that threaten the quality of many present day breeds, then it will have served a useful purpose.

Although you might find it difficult to put into words what you are looking for in good movement, it may be that you have sensed it without knowing why. It may be just the feeling of pleasure over the flashy gait of a stylish entry in the show ring, or the thrill of excitement that comes with watching a hunting dog work smoothly across a field and suddenly freeze on point. You may instinctively have sensed the importance of stamina if you have hunted over a retriever that swims strongly and eagerly at the close of a strenuous day in the marshes. Or, if you are one who has handled a willing dog through obedience competition where advanced training demands constant effort in jumping, you have experienced the need for soundness.

Too often puppies are selected solely on the basis of their expression, personality, color, coat texture, or size-traits, which to be sure, give each its special appeal and add to the joy of the owner. But these traits alone are not enough. Structure must also be considered if a breed or a strain is to be kept strong. So it is to the breeders who know what to look for and what to avoid, who know what makes a good dog move well and why, that novices should turn for guidance and learning. Experience is a good teacher, but knowledge-with a little luck!-steers the shortest way to lasting success.

Who knows—this dog just *might* be your own!

BIBLIOGRAPHY

ALL OWNERS of pure-bred dogs will benefit themselves and their dogs by enriching their knowledge of breeds and of canine care, training, breeding, psychology and other important aspects of dog management. The following list of books covers further reading recommended by judges, veterinarians, breeders, trainers and other authorities. Books may be obtained at the finer book stores and pet shops, or through Howell Book House Inc., publishers, New York.

Breed Books

AFGHAN HOUND, Complete	Miller & Gilbert
AIREDALE, New Complete	Edwards
ALASKAN MALAMUTE, Complete	Riddle & Seeley
BASSET HOUND, Complete	Braun
BEAGLE, Complete	Noted Authorities
BLOODHOUND, Complete	Brey & Reed
BOXER, Complete	Denlinger
BRITTANY SPANIEL, Complete	Riddle
BULLDOG, New Complete	Hanes
BULL TERRIER, New Complete	Eberhard
CAIRN TERRIER, Complete	Marvin
CHESAPEAKE BAY RETRIEVER, Complete	Cherry
CHIHUAHUA, Complete	Noted Authorities
COCKER SPANIEL, New	Kraeuchi
COLLIE, Complete	Official Publication of the Collie Club of America
DACHSHUND, The New	Meistrell
DALMATIAN, The	Treen
DOBERMAN PINSCHER, New	Walker
ENGLISH SETTER, New Complete	Tuck & Howell
ENGLISH SPRINGER SPANIEL, New	Goodall & Gasow
FOX TERRIER, New Complete	Silvernail
GERMAN SHEPHERD DOG, Complete	Bennett
GERMAN SHORTHAIRED POINTER, New	Maxwell
GOLDEN RETRIEVER, Complete	Fischer
GREAT DANE, New Complete	Noted Authorities
GREAT PYRENEES, Complete	Strang & Giffin
IRISH SETTER, New	Thompson
IRISH WOLFHOUND, Complete	Starbuck
KEESHOND, Complete	Peterson
LABRADOR RETRIEVER, Complete	Warwick
LHASA APSO, Complete	Herbel
MINIATURE SCHNAUZER, Complete	Eskrigge
NEWFOUNDLAND, New Complete	Chern
NORWEGIAN ELKHOUND, New Complete	Wallo
OLD ENGLISH SHEEPDOG, Complete	Mandeville
PEKINGESE, Quigley Book of	Quigley
PEMBROKE WELSH CORGI, Complete	Sargent & Harper
POMERANIAN, New Complete	Ricketts
POODLE, New Complete	Hopkins & Irick
POODLE CLIPPING AND GROOMING BOOK, Complete	Kalstone
PUG, Complete	Trullinger
PULI, Complete	Owen
ST. BERNARD, New Complete	Noted Authorities, rev. Raulston
SAMOYED, Complete	Ward
SCHIPPERKE, Official Book of	Root, Martin, Kent
SCOTTISH TERRIER, Complete	Marvin
SHETLAND SHEEPDOG, The New	Riddle
SHIH TZU, The (English)	Dadds
SIBERIAN HUSKY, Complete	Demidoff
TERRIERS, The Book of All	Marvin
WEST HIGHLAND WHITE TERRIER, Complete	Marvin
WHIPPET, Complete	Pegram
YORKSHIRE TERRIER, Complete	Gordon & Bennett

Breeding

ART OF BREEDING BETTER DOGS, New	Onsott
BREEDING YOUR SHOW DOG, Joy of	Seranne
HOW TO BREED DOGS	Whitney
HOW PUPPIES ARE BORN	Prine
INHERITANCE OF COAT COLOR IN DOGS	Little

Care and Training

DOG OBEDIENCE, Complete Book of	Saunders
NOVICE, OPEN AND UTILITY COURSES	Saunders
DOG CARE AND TRAINING FOR BOYS AND GIRLS	Saunders
DOG NUTRITION, Collins Guide to	Collins
DOG TRAINING FOR KIDS	Benjamin
DOG TRAINING, Koehler Method of	Koehler
GO FIND! Training Your Dog to Track	Davis
GUARD DOG TRAINING, Koehler Method of	Koehler
OPEN OBEDIENCE FOR RING, HOME AND FIELD, Koehler Method of	Koehler
SPANIELS FOR SPORT (English)	Radcliffe
SUCCESSFUL DOG TRAINING, The Pearsall Guide to	Pearsall
TOY DOGS, Kalstone Guide to Grooming All	Kalstone
TRAINING THE RETRIEVER	Kersley
TRAINING YOUR DOG TO WIN OBEDIENCE TITLES,	Morsell
TRAIN YOUR OWN GUN DOG, How to	Goodall
UTILITY DOG TRAINING, Koehler Method of	Koehler
VETERINARY HANDBOOK, Dog Owner's Home	Carlson & Giffin

General

COMPLETE DOG BOOK, The	Official Publication of American Kennel Club
DISNEY ANIMALS, World of	Koehler
DOG IN ACTION, The	Lyon
DOG BEHAVIOR, New Knowledge of	Pfaffenberger
DOG JUDGE'S HANDBOOK	Tietjen
DOG JUDGING, Nicholas Guide to	Nicholas
DOG PEOPLE ARE CRAZY	Riddle
DOG PSYCHOLOGY	Whitney
DOG STANDARDS ILLUSTRATED	
DOGSTEPS, Illustrated Gait at a Glance	Elliott
ENCYCLOPEDIA OF DOGS, International	Dangerfield, Howell & Riddle
JUNIOR SHOWMANSHIP HANDBOOK	Brown & Mason
MY TIMES WITH DOGS	Fletcher
OUR PUPPY'S BABY BOOK (blue or pink)	
RICHES TO BITCHES	Shattuck
SUCCESSFUL DOG SHOWING, Forsyth Guide to	Forsyth
TRIM, GROOM AND SHOW YOUR DOG, How to	Saunders
WHY DOES YOUR DOG DO THAT?	Bergman
WILD DOGS in Life and Legend	Riddle
WORLD OF SLED DOGS, From Siberia to Sport Racing	Coppinger

References:

Bracket, Lloyd C. and Horswell, Laurence A., "The Dog in Motion", *Dog World Magazine* (U.S.A.), August 1961–October 1965.
The Canine, A Veterinary Aid in Anatomical Transparencies, Fromm Laboratories, Inc., Grafton, Wisconsin, 1967.
Ellenberger, Baum, Dittrich, *An Atlas of Animal Anatomy for Artists,* Dover Publications, Inc., New York.
Lyon, McDowell, *The Dog in Action,* 1950, Howell Book House Inc., New York.
Muybridge, Eadweard, *Animals in Motion,* 1957, Dover Publications, Inc., New York.
Smythe, R. H., *The Conformation of the Dog,* 1957, Popular Dogs Publishing Co., London.
Smythe, R. H., *The Anatomy of Dog Breeding,* Popular Dogs Publishing Co., London, 1962.
Smythe, R. H., *Dog Structure and Movement,* Popular Dogs Publishing Co., London, 1970.
Stillman, J. D. B., *The Horse in Motion,* 1882, James R. Osgood and Co., Boston.
"Stonehenge", *The Dogs of the British Islands,* Second Edition, 1872, London.